"Dive into Amanda Morgan's new book, *Not Just Cute: How Powerful Play Drives Development in Early Childhood* to truly discover the power and value of play. Amanda will inspire you to think, reflect and take action as a promoter of rich and meaningful play for young children. This book is a gem!"

-**Kathy Gallo** and **LeeAnn Soucy**, The Two Pushy Dames, Education Consultants

"As an early childhood educator, I know firsthand how challenging it can be to explain the deep, meaningful learning that happens through play. In *Not Just Cute,* Amanda Morgan brings both the heart and the science to the conversation, equipping educators with the confidence and language to advocate for what we know is best for young children. Amanda's passion for play-based learning shines on every page, offering teachers and parents the understanding and encouragement we all need. This is not just a book — it's an essential guide for anyone who wants to nurture true, lasting growth in children."

-**Deborah J. Stewart**, M.Ed., Creator of Teach Preschool, Author of *Ready for Kindergarten*

"Amanda Morgan has written the book early childhood programs have been waiting for. *Not Just Cute* is both accessible and academically grounded, giving parents, educators, and leaders the tools they need to defend—and deliver—what's best for young children. This is more than a book; it's a call to action for anyone committed to teaching and raising healthier, happier, and more resilient kids."

-**Dr. Michele Borba**, Educational Psychologist, Author of *Thrivers* and *UnSelfie*

"Child development specialist Amanda Morgan contends that people can't support what they don't understand. With that in mind, she uses research, her many years of experience, and an easygoing, conversational style to help people understand why all children need to play!"

-**Rae Pica**, Early Childhood Advocate, Author of *Why Play? How to Make Play an Essential Part of Early Education*

"Amanda Morgan is a fierce advocate for play in early childhood education, and in her new meticulously researched book, she explains why. Point by point, supported by research, Morgan leads readers to understand the power of play, the detrimental effects of its absence, and gives practical advice that teachers and administrators can implement immediately. This is a must-read!"

-**Allison McDonald**, Creator of No Time For Flash Cards, Author of *Everyday Preschool in the Classroom*

"A Game-Changer for Early Childhood Educators! This book doesn't just celebrate play—it explains why it matters, how it supports development, and why it's at the heart of every high-quality early learning experience. If you're ready to move beyond outdated expectations and embrace the true power of play, this book is for you. It will leave you feeling as if you finally have the secret recipe that will take your early learning program to the next level while still honoring how young children learn best, through play."

-**Vanessa Levin**, Creator, Pre-K Pages, Author of *Teach Smarter*

NOT JUST CUTE

NOT JUST CUTE

How Powerful Play Drives Development in Early Childhood

AMANDA MORGAN

Foreword by
Dale C. Farran, PhD
Emerita Professor, Vanderbilt University

Published by Amanda Morgan, Not Just Cute LLC.

ISBN: 979-8-218-66593-7

LCCN: In Process

Book cover designed by Frances Anne Elopre.

Cover image from Adobe Stock by New Africa.

Illustrations by author using Canva Pro.

Author photo by Three Seas Photography.

Contact: amanda@notjustcute.com

For my husband Steve, who has always believed there were books for me to write. And in memory of his father, Vern, who filled his life and family with love and play.

Contents

Author's Note

Not Just Cute was written with multiple audiences in mind. Its language is conversational and accessible, while also offering the notes and citations to support deep academic inquiry. If this book opens your eyes to new ideas—or simply gives you the research-based language to articulate what you've always known—please pass it on to someone else in your educational community. Whether it lands in the hands of a brand-new teacher, a seasoned administrator, a curious parent, or a skeptical board member, my hope is that *Not Just Cute* helps us all get on the same page, grounded in research and united by what's best for young children.

Because in the end, no matter our roles, we all share the same goal: to build a brighter future by giving every child the joyful, meaningful, and developmentally rich learning experiences they deserve. Let's get to work—our youngest learners are counting on us.

Foreword

By Dale C. Farran, PhD

Amanda Morgan's excellent book on the power of play provides parents and teachers alike with a short, highly informative primer on understanding the role play has in the brain development of young children and the critical importance of reversing the current trend toward viewing play as nonessential.

As Amanda points out, over the past 25 years or so, we changed our notions of the experiences young children need in order to develop. The result of this changed view, intended or otherwise, has been an increasingly popular belief that young children, ages 3–5 years, need focused academic instruction to get them ready for school. This belief is misguided.

Developmental researchers have long called attention to the critical importance of early childhood experiences as ones that need to be safe and affirming, offer many chances to independently explore indoors and outdoors, and strongly favor small group interactions and hands-on active learning over large group, teacher-led instruction. Early childhood programs are increasingly accountable for teaching concrete school readiness skills, primarily early literacy.

Yet, neither developmental theory nor any rigorous evaluation supports a narrow focus on basic academic skill training as a substitute for truly enriched early childhood experiences. In fact, evaluations of skill-focused preschool interventions indicate that academic gains are not long-lasting. One rigorous evaluation of a statewide pre-K program provided troubling findings of long-term negative effects on both achievement and behavior. (I am one of the directors of this state study.)

With evidence of both fadeout and negative effects, now is a good time to pause, take stock, and ask: are we doing this right? Amanda's book provides important guidance for a much-needed change in direction.

During early childhood, on average, about two-thirds of the body's calories are involved in brain growth and functioning, while this ratio is closer to one-third by mid-adolescence. A wealth of neuroscience evidence demonstrates that the developing brain is highly malleable in early childhood, with consequences for brain structure and function. Important environmental factors include nutrition, level and quality of cognitive and language stimulation, abundance of learning opportunities through exploration and new experiences, freedom from chronic or extreme stressors, and social-emotional support from caregivers. These early experiences result in lasting effects on brain regions and circuitry highly involved in such important areas as self-regulation, language, memory, and attention.

Recent advances in neuroscience concern the developmental mechanisms and processes of growth in children's brains. Critically important is the fact that the human brain evolved as an active processor of information, prepared to learn from new experiences and environments. As one neuroscientist put it: "The brain evolved to control action. The brain is an action-oriented and not a perception-oriented system." What this means is what any parent will tell you—children need to move; they need to act on their environments and learn from the results!

Young children actively search for relationships in their environments, and their spontaneous play is often organized and directed in ways to support effective learning about cause and effect. Indeed, 2-, 3-, and 4-year-old children come to clever causal understandings through simply observing patterns, in some cases arriving at more efficient solutions than those of college students. Interestingly, however, overly direct teaching from adults may interfere with rather than facilitate children's active thinking.

One set of research studies found that efficient solutions to problems involving cause and effect were dependent on the adult taking a more naïve role (e.g., "I don't know how this toy works, let's find out."). If the adult said she owned the toy and was going to teach the child how to use it, children mimicked the "correct" solution and failed to find more efficient solutions such as the ones they demonstrated when the adult acted naïvely, and children explored on their own.

Creating more opportunities for active engagement in problem solving, exploration, and investigation requires a shift in how we engage children. Problem solving and learning through exploration, by definition, occur most easily in small group interactions. Moreover, adults must invest time in developing exploratory activities and changing them to maintain children's interest. Moving away from an emphasis on basic skills instruction means that teachers and parents will have to value and prioritize creating activities that promote exploration and engage children in active problem solving. It takes determination and commitment to do so, and by doing so, deeper learning will occur.

Working memory and selective sustained attention are important competencies developing during early childhood. Both working memory and attention are important for maintaining children's engagement in learning. One of the earlier, highly referenced studies examining the development of attention across the preschool years found a 98% increase in focused attention during free play between 2.5 and 3.5 years. Only free play brought about this increase in focused attention.

The single-minded focus on academic preparedness has led to children spending much less time in outdoor activities, and while it may seem counterintuitive, good evidence suggests that more physical exercise, especially outdoors, leads to greater focused attention during learning activities. Outdoor time (more than a few minutes and not prescribed physical education) provides time for children to explore, switching back and forth between effortless and effortful attention. In fact, some researchers assert that the ages of 4-6 years may be the period most vulnerable to negative effects from not being outdoors enough, including negative effects on the development of sustained, selective attention.

In summary, neuroscience evidence does not support highly-structured, academically rigid "schools" for young children, whether they are facing economic risk or not. But, this concept of "school" is, in fact, more and more what public and private preschools look like. Best practice for early childhood development minimizes the role of teacher/adult directed learning in favor of environments structured to provide opportunities for active learning such as interesting materials, access to the natural world, chances for peer interaction and collaboration, and child-directed play. Children need to actively explore and experiment on their surroundings. In such environments adults are not laissez-faire; rather they scaffold those experiences through conversations, adapting learning challenges to individual children's development, and providing explanations that lead children toward generalizable principles about their worlds.

Now is the time to create these types of early childhood experiences. With the rapid expansion of public funding for early childhood education, it is critical to rescue classrooms from an inappropriate narrow focus on basic school readiness skills. It is time for developmental science to be taken seriously; the costs for children of not making these changes will be great and long-lasting.

Dale C. Farran, PhD, *is an emerita professor at Vanderbilt University and a director in the Tennessee Voluntary Prekindergarten Study. She has been extensively involved in landmark early childhood research, including the Abecedarian Project and work with Kamehameha Schools. With over 100 peer-reviewed publications, her career has been dedicated to evaluating early childhood programs and services, with a focus on helping children from low-income families achieve positive outcomes in education and life.*

CHAPTER 1

A Pre-K Paradox

What if a program designed to help children succeed in school was actually setting them back? That's exactly what researchers uncovered in the Tennessee Voluntary Prekindergarten study—one of the most eye-opening studies in early childhood education.[1] As Tennessee expanded its state pre-K program in 2009 and 2010, they found there were far more families interested in enrolling their children than they could accommodate. As a result, children throughout the state were randomly assigned a spot in their local pre-K programs, and others were not.

Researchers like Dr. Dale Farran realized they had an opportunity rarely found in social science—a large, randomized controlled trial. This study involved nearly 3,000 children across Tennessee, with half randomly assigned to pre-K and half left out—much like the flip of a coin. This created a rare, gold-standard research opportunity: a way to measure the true impact of pre-K without outside factors like family income or education level skewing the results.

Researchers expected this study to confirm what many already believed: Pre-K gives children an early advantage. They hoped strong data would lead to more funding, more programs, and more opportunities for young learners. But what they found shocked them.

Surprising Results: Controversy & Curiosity

After the pre-K year, children who participated in the pre-K program scored higher than children who didn't. Just what you'd expect to find, right? But that difference disappeared after the two groups converged for their kindergarten year. That may have been disappointing, but not too surprising; a "fadeout" effect is often observed in early childhood research, and is one of the pesky puzzles researchers often wrestle with.[2] Where this study really started making waves was with the follow-up data.

By third grade, the children who attended pre-K were falling behind. Not only did their math and science scores not keep up with their peers who hadn't attended—they were significantly *worse*. By sixth grade, the gap had grown, and the pre-K group fell behind in English language arts scores as well.[3] Even more troubling, they were facing higher rates of disciplinary issues and school expulsions. The very program designed to help them succeed seemed to be working against them.

At the beginning of the study, researchers believed they would gather definitive proof of the benefits of early childhood education—solid evidence to advocate for more funding and expansion. But instead of celebrating, they found themselves scrambling to explain unexpected results. What went wrong? And more importantly—what were they missing?

The response was swift and severe. Headlines and editorials claimed "Pre-K Harms Kids." Lead researcher Dr. Dale Farran said she even had colleagues asking, "When did Dale stop loving children?" as they assumed her research would actually detract from early childhood education efforts.[4]

Pressured to underplay or hide the results, Farran instead got curious and dug into the research to find out what could be learned. "It really has required a lot of soul-searching, a lot of reading of the literature to try to think of what were plausible reasons that might account for this," she admitted in an interview with NPR.[5]

"I thought, well, this is called science," she later told me on my podcast.[6] "Shouldn't we be grappling with the fact of these issues and not trying to make them go away or just hide them and say we don't believe them?"

She, and others like her, began looking for what was different about this study. They all knew the body of research dating back to the 1960s and 1970s, which showed significant positive benefits from other early childhood programs.[7] Why not this one?

The Missing Ingredients: What's Changed in Preschool?

Science teaches us that when an experiment yields unexpected results, we examine the ingredients. Water is H_2O—two parts hydrogen, one part oxygen. Remove the oxygen, and you don't just get a different liquid. You get hydrogen gas—highly flammable and dangerous. A missing element changes everything. The same is true for early childhood education.

Perhaps baking is a better analogy for some of us. It's a more accessible kind of chemistry. You can take a lot of creative liberty with a chocolate cake recipe—adjust the salt, swap ingredients, add chocolate chips—but take out the chocolate, and it's not a chocolate cake anymore. You can make an eggless chocolate cake or a flourless chocolate cake, but there's no such thing as a chocolate-less chocolate cake. The key ingredient defines the whole thing. The same goes for early childhood education: Take out what matters most, and you change the entire outcome.

If early childhood research shows a different outcome from what is expected, we have to analyze the ingredients put into the programs. Similar to chemistry and baking, you can't leave out key ingredients of quality early education and expect the same results. Even worse, without the key ingredients, you might find something destructive. In our metaphors, it was flammable hydrogen gas, or a (tragically, in my opinion) chocolate-free dessert. In Tennessee it was young children whose early education experience negatively impacted the trajectory of their schooling and possibly their lives for the long-term.[8]

And so, instead of providing conclusive evidence for the developmental benefits of the state pre-K program, the Tennessee pre-K study produced a central question: With all the variation inherent in creating early childhood programs, what are the key ingredients that must be included in order to be effective?

Dr. Farran isn't the only one trying to determine what's missing from today's early childhood programs. When eight researchers penned a working paper with the title, "Why are Preschool Programs Becoming Less Effective?", you'd better believe I printed out a hard copy and sat down with my highlighter in hand, entranced as though it was the latest best-selling novel.[9]

Their titular question comes from this observation:

When examining 17 notable studies on preschool programs over the past several decades, programs beginning between 1960 and 1999 showed impacts that were twice as large as those from programs beginning between 2000 and 2011. Additionally, the later programs seemed to show more of a fadeout effect than those from the earlier decades.

Put more simply, a review of the research showed that modern preschool programs yielded smaller, shorter-lasting benefits than those running before the year 2000.

So, while nearly every proposal for funding an early childhood education program will cite research from the "gold standard" programs of the 1960s and 1970s—Perry Preschool and Abecedarian—few, if any, are replicating their results today. We should all be asking exactly what these researchers asked—What's going on?

The paper's authors noted that there are many factors to consider when looking at diminishing impact. In my reading, I saw these factors fitting into two categories, a classic case of good news and bad news.

Here's the good news:

The impact of public early childhood interventions is smaller, in part, because of other successful interventions. Improvements in nutrition, health, and parent support since the 1960s have elevated child outcomes across the board. While disparities remain, children generally begin preschool programs today with a stronger foundation—meaning the programs' relative impact is smaller. A rising tide lifts all boats, and while that manifests in studies as a blunted effect from preschool programs, in this case, that's actually a win.

Now for the bad news:

The second category of reasoning the panel suggests examining is the content and methods of modern pre-K programs. They note the HOW and the WHAT of early education have both changed dramatically, and that could be why programs simply aren't as effective. Earlier programs like Perry Preschool and Abecedarian, and many others pre-2000, focused on the whole child—building social skills, emotional regulation, and curiosity alongside academic foundations. But today's programs have shifted. Instead of nurturing development through rich, play-based experiences, many have succumbed to "academic push-down," treating young children like miniature elementary students by pushing expectations and content down to younger and younger grades. And research is showing that this shift is actually hurting more than helping.

As the paper's authors point out, "The almost complete fadeout of today's preschool programs in RCT (randomized controlled trial) studies suggests that focusing on early literacy and, perhaps, numeracy skills in preschool programs, at best, is ineffective and may also result in negative outcomes in the medium-term for children."

To be clear, this doesn't mean that these early academic skills can't be included (in fact, they very much *should* be), but if they've become the primary *focus*, there's been a trade-off. As there's been more and more pushed down, something else has been pushed out. And based on the results of this research team's meta-analysis, it would seem that whatever has been pushed out, is a key ingredient for quality early education. One we need to put back into the equation.

Play: An Essential Ingredient

High-quality early education isn't just about early academics—it's about nurturing the whole child through rich, meaningful play experiences. Yet, play is precisely what's missing from many modern programs. In this book, I'll make the argument (with the help of distinguished researchers in the fields of psychology, child development, and education) that play is a key ingredient in any high-quality early childhood program, one that has been increasingly pushed out of today's early childhood programs, at the expense of our youngest learners.

Play is not just cute. It's not extra. It's not what we do *after* the "real learning" is finished. Play is where the real learning happens. When we allow it to be pushed out of early childhood, we're not just reshaping school—we're reshaping children's futures. Whether you're a teacher, administrator, policymaker, or parent, I hope the information you find here will help you to better understand, support, and advocate for play. You have the power to protect this essential part of learning. And the research is clear: If we want children to thrive, we must put play back where it belongs—at the heart of early childhood education.

Key Takeaways:

- The Tennessee pre-K study found that early academic gains **faded and reversed** over time.
- Past early education models (e.g., Perry Preschool) were more **play-based** and had **lasting benefits**.
- **Play is essential** for whole-child development—its removal may explain declining pre-K effectiveness.

Reflect:

- **Why** do you think early academic skills alone don't lead to long-term success?
- **How** does play contribute to social, emotional, and cognitive growth in ways didactic methods do not?

Take Action:

- **Observe** a pre-K classroom. What is the role of play?
- **Advocate** for play in your learning community. Simply **recognizing and thanking** current sources is a great start!
- **Share** this research with educators and policymakers.

CHAPTER 2

People Don't Value What They Don't Understand

In my work helping people better understand and better articulate the importance of play, there's a phrase I come back to over and over again: People don't value what they don't understand. Notice I did NOT say people don't value play when they're horrible people or when they hate children. No, people simply don't value what they don't understand.

For me, valuing play is an obvious choice. I've studied play and play-based practices for decades. I've read research and I've seen first-hand evidence. I've spent a long time coming to understand things about play that make it very easy for me to see how important it is for young children and their development. Maybe you relate to that. But not everyone has had the same experiences. And if someone sees play as a fun way to take a break from "real" learning, or even sees it as a frivolous waste of time, I don't view that as a personal flaw. I simply recognize there are some pieces of information they're missing, and that's skewed their valuation. Because people just don't value what they don't understand.

I've fallen into this trap myself. Let me give you a quick story as an example. I have four boys with lots of energy. A few years back, a neighbor asked if they wanted to earn some money clearing noxious weeds from his property. They worked HARD for several days wielding pickaxes and shovels and levers to remove these stubborn weeds, some of which had grown taller than they were at the time. They were excited about the opportunity to earn money, and I was excited to watch from my kitchen window and see them put all that big energy to good use.

Well, one day, that neighbor dropped by and handed me an envelope to pay the boys for their work. I was running late, as I often am, so I quickly thanked him and headed to grab my purse and keys and get going to wherever it was I was supposed to be. As I did, I thought to myself that this envelope felt odd. It didn't feel like a check or a few bills. So, I took a peek inside before setting it on my counter.

There, I found one large coin. A single Canadian coin, in fact—and we live in the U.S.! Then, I saw that it said twenty dollars on it. OK, that was better than finding what I originally thought was a dollar coin, but still—it was A LOT of really hard work. Twenty Canadian dollars split between four boys seemed off. I was so confused. But I was already supposed to be on my way, so I just set it down and headed out.

The whole time I was away I kept thinking, "What is going on? This is so weird. Why would he pay for all that work with 20 Canadian dollars?" I didn't value it, because I didn't understand. There were some key pieces of information I needed to have in order to properly value this coin.

Finally, it dawned on me that maybe I was missing something. When I got home, I looked at the coin more carefully. And then I Googled it. Turns out, it was pure gold—a collector's coin. And it was worth, not twenty dollars, but several HUNDRED dollars. He had actually paid them very generously, and my boys were thrilled!

I didn't misunderstand the value on purpose or because I felt like being difficult; I just didn't have the context to really understand it. The actual value of the coin didn't change. The facts were always the facts. But my new understanding of those facts helped me to finally value it properly.[1]

Play: Misunderstood and Undervalued

Just like my misunderstanding of the coin's value, many people misunderstand the value of play. They see it as fun but optional, rather than as an essential driver of development. People who question the value of play in our early childhood environments are likely not trying to be difficult or to steal joy or to ruin childhood. They simply can't properly value what they don't fully understand. The good news is, once we help fill in the gaps of that understanding—once they catch the vision of the true value of play for young children—they often become advocates right alongside us.

One of the most impactful examples I've observed of how understanding play transforms perspectives comes from a program working directly with parents and caregivers—Play Smart Literacy in Chicago. Founded by Michelle Dinneen-White, this community outreach program serves areas of the city impacted by deep poverty with the mission of educating parents and caregivers about the power of play and conversation in the lives of young children.

At first, many caregivers are skeptical. They may ask, "Isn't my child too young to learn real skills?" or say, "Play is just play—learning happens in school." Their concerns aren't rooted in opposition but in a lack of information. As the workshops unfold, however, their perspectives shift. They quickly see firsthand how small, everyday moments—playing with blocks, singing a song, talking about colors at the grocery store—lay the foundation for language, problem-solving, and social skills. They begin to realize: Play is powerful. Play is learning.

What makes Play Smart Literacy especially influential is the fact that many of its outreach leaders once shared those same doubts. Brenda Lopez and Cecilia Gutierrez, two of the program's parent educators, weren't always passionate about play. They used to believe that real learning happened in classrooms where children sat still, listening and memorizing. But once they experienced the impact of play with their own children, everything changed. Seeing how powerful it was to play, talk, and learn with their own children, they became almost evangelical about spreading the good word of play with as many families and caregivers as possible.

Unlike traditional programs that expect families to seek them out, Play Smart Literacy is fully mobile. They go to where the families are—playgrounds, laundromats, gas stations, markets, and schools. With simple mini lessons and hands-on demonstrations, they show caregivers how everyday interactions—stacking cups, narrating a child's actions, asking playful questions—support brain development. They don't just explain the importance of play; they model it, right there in the moment. Like missionaries of play, they talk to anyone with a child in their lives and follow up with them for months or even years.

For Brenda and Cecilia, this work is personal. Their own transformation fuels their passion. Talking about this work, their faces light up.

"I didn't know that talk and play can make my child's development...better," Cecilia shared when I interviewed her and other members of the team on *Not Just Cute: The Podcast.* [2] "I wish I knew that before, when I was younger."

Brenda echoed that sentiment. "I realized that I wasn't the only parent that didn't know that you could add words to play. It gets me really excited when...parents don't know that, and I'm like, 'OK...now you have access to that information.' So even if my kids didn't have that when they were babies...I'm happy that now I'm able to help other parents know (what) I wish I would have known."

These amazing advocates didn't value play earlier simply because they didn't know then what they know today. Which is why they now pour their time and energy into getting that message to other families sooner.

Once someone's eyes are open to the science and developmental power of play, they become the biggest advocates. Their advocacy starts a ripple effect. And that ripple effect can become a movement.

I've seen this firsthand as I've worked with teams to better serve children by supporting their play. As Kris Ramos, a program director in Houston, told me about her team's response to focusing on play for their team's professional development: "It's become our whole culture...our whole personality of our program."

Kris' school had been "play-based" for 43 years, but that term meant different things to different people on the team. There were good things happening, but there were inconsistencies and insecurities across the team.

"They knew that what we were doing was good for kids, but they didn't necessarily have the 'why.' They needed the research and the facts to confidently defend it to others, advocate for it, explain it, and take it a little bit deeper."

That changed when Kris' team dove into my training on powerful play. Once her team began to get on the same page about play, she noticed an immediate shift. Not only did her teachers gain the vocabulary and research to articulate why play matters, but they began to see themselves—and their work—in a new light. Their confidence soared, and so did the quality of the classroom experiences they provided.

Once they *knew* better, they decided to *do* better.

Kris reflected on her team's renewed passion, "We're all the time growing, nonstop. It's...our purpose. We're all in. And it's been really, really enjoyable."

So, if you feel that people aren't valuing play, or if, perhaps, *you* don't quite see the value in play-based education, then that isn't a character flaw and we don't need to be enemies. It simply means there's a gap in understanding. There's some piece of information that is needed to make that connection.

People don't value what they don't understand. So, let's help people—including ourselves—to better understand why we play. This book is here to help us bridge that gap in understanding. It aims to give us the words, the research, and the stories that help us not just to defend play—but to inspire others to embrace it, too.

Key Takeaways:

- People often **dismiss** play's importance because they don't fully **understand** its developmental benefits.
- Understanding transforms **skepticism into advocacy**—once people see play's power, they become its strongest supporters.

Reflect:

- **Recall** a time when you misunderstood the value of something? How did your perspective change?
- **What strategies** have been effective in shifting educators' and parents' views on play-based learning?

Take Action:

- **Observe** how play is perceived in your school or community. **Create** messaging that could help shift the conversation.
- **Engage** in conversations that highlight real-world examples of play's impact on children's growth.

CHAPTER 3

Defining Play

Before we jump into why play not only matters, but is a powerful driver of learning and development for young children, we have to define what play is. And that has proven to be a bit tricky.

It may be tempting to think play is just a simple thing and should therefore be a simple thing to define, but many experts and groups offer slightly different perspectives from each other when it comes to nailing down a precise definition. It's actually a pretty lively topic of discussion in the academic world!

In many other scholarly conversations, definitions are more clear-cut. Chemists agree that water is always H_2O.

Math scholars agree that in the Pythagorean theorem, a squared plus b squared always equals c squared. Biologists and high school students everywhere all know that the mitochondria is the powerhouse of the cell—even if most of us still aren't exactly sure what that means! But there isn't one, easy definition for play that everyone universally agrees on.

Consider the definition of a square. Easy, right? It has four straight, equal sides and four right angles.

Now, how would you define the color blue? Or love? Or beauty?

When does something stop being blue and start being purple? Where's the exact point that friendship becomes love or beauty becomes breathtaking?

It seems defining play—at least in English—is more like defining the second group of words—blue, love, or beauty—than it's like defining a square. There's something amorphous about it—not in the sense that it isn't real (love and beauty and the color blue are all definitely very real), but in the way that it can permeate different moments and take on different shapes. Yet there are core elements that remain the same.

So, let's take a look at just a few of those definitions, and see if we can tease out some core elements.

Core Components of Play: Agency & Joy

Psychologist Peter Gray defines play as self-chosen and self-directed; intrinsically motivated—more means than ends; guided by mental rules; always creative, usually imaginative.[1]

As you'll learn in the next chapter, Dr. Gray led a group of researchers connecting the decline in play to the decline in mental health for children.[2] A key part of that tandem decline, they assert, is the lack of agency, self-efficacy, or the belief that the self—the child in this case—has power to choose, control, and direct important aspects of their own lives. Can you see that common thread of agency running through Gray's definition of play?

Self-chosen and self-directed is certainly a reflection of agency, or the power to choose and to act.

Intrinsically motivated, again, reflects that internal locus of control, that the motivation comes from within rather than externally.

Guided by mental rules means that there are self-imposed boundaries for the play. The block structure is a barn for horses, because the child decided that's what it would be. The child playing the baby in dramatic play will crawl on the floor and talk in baby talk because that's what the child perceives a baby would do, and those are the rules of playing a baby. Those mental rules, again, reflect that internal work of deciding, defining, and being motivated.

And at the bottom of the list: creative and imaginative. Creative endeavors are, again, a perfect expression of agency. As a child creates and imagines, they get absolute control, in an absolutely appropriate way.

So, we have agency as one essential component.

Now, let's look at a definition from psychiatrist and clinical researcher, Dr. Stuart Brown. (No, you don't have to have a color for your last name in order to study play, but it seems to have worked out for these two.) After a distinguished, decades-long career, Dr. Brown has defined play this way:

"It's voluntary, it's pleasurable, it offers a sense of engagement, it takes you out of time. And the act itself is more important than the outcome."[3]

Dr. Brown's definition includes the same agency accentuated in Dr. Gray's definition, but it also has a strong emphasis on the sense of joy—it's pleasurable and it takes you out of time—which is to say you lose track of time because it's not a chore, you're not counting the minutes until you can quit. You do it because you enjoy it.

Even if you're frustrated in the moment—because the puzzle is hard, or the blocks keep falling, or your friends don't want to play the same way you do—there's an immense sense of joy as you continue, overcome, and resolve those issues. There's a satisfaction that drives you.

Of course, joy can be tricky to define and measure. What brings you joy may be different from what brings your neighbor joy. In fact, what brings you joy today may be different from what brought you joy fifteen years ago. And that explains why the way we play is individual. I may see going for a run as play and going shopping as work, while someone else would define those tasks the other way around. We all have different preferences because what brings us joy is personal. *Play is personal.*

Because of that, it's not hard to imagine two children in the same context, and one is enjoying a playful experience while the other is not. Let's imagine children playing soccer. Sounds like that would be play, right? Well, imagine one loves soccer. She's playing and kicking and practicing all the time—no one has to make her do it; she just chooses to because she enjoys it so much. The motivation comes from inside her. When she's out there on the pitch, of course she's working hard and trying to score a goal and win the game, but she also just loves playing.

Now imagine another child playing soccer. He doesn't want to do it, but his parents are "making" him. They drag him out to practice where he counts the minutes until he's done. The one saving grace is that when he scores a goal, his parents promise to buy him ice cream, so at least he has that to look forward to.

Now, whether or not it's worthwhile to encourage children to do things they don't want to do is a whole other discussion, but can you see how one scenario is play and the other probably isn't?

When it comes to play in our classrooms, we need to realize that the children won't all experience play opportunities the same way. Some children will dive right into a sensory experience and we'll see all that agency, motivation, and joy, while another child will stand by and watch...probably with a look of disgust on their face because putting their hands in THAT stuff does not sound fun at all. Or you may have children who would LIVE in the dramatic play area all day, every day, creating stories and constructing worlds, and other children who would prefer to quietly tinker with intricate puzzles or arrange loose parts.

Like love, beauty, and the color blue, play is best understood through experience. To define it, we must rely not only on research but also on careful observation of how children engage with it.

Play as a Spectrum

So, between Dr. Gray and Dr. Brown, we have two essential themes for a definition of play—agency and joy. One challenge in defining play is, like the definitions of love and beauty and even the color blue, part of play's definition is dependent on how it's experienced...*personally*. This makes observation and responsiveness imperative.

The other challenge is that play, much like these other examples, also exists on a spectrum. Consider the spectrum of love. Where do you put the love you feel for your favorite neighbor vs your favorite song vs your favorite pizza? You may refer to each by saying, "Oh, I LOVE that one," but the experience is different. Similarly, consider the things you consider "beautiful." A painting, a person, a sunset, a moment—they are all beautiful, yet not the same.

And the color blue may be hard to define without having seen it, but even if you've seen something called "blue," there's still a whole spectrum of tones that are all called blue. Light blue, baby blue, cornflower blue, cobalt blue, royal blue, sapphire blue, indigo blue, navy blue... If you go to a paint store and just ask for the color "blue," they'll likely hand you a book with hundreds of samples, each one slightly different from the other. And all along that blue spectrum, there's no place where the color isn't blue—even though each one is different from the colors next to it.

Similarly, research from Jennifer Zosh, Kathy Hirsh-Pasek, and their colleagues highlights the way play in learning environments unfolds along a spectrum, rather than fitting into a single definition.[4] Much like the varying shades of blue on a color spectrum, different forms of play exist at every point on the Spectrum of Playful Learning—each slightly different from the other, but each still play. From this perspective, there isn't one form of play that is morally better than the others (an interesting argument play advocates tend to get tangled into). Instead, the "best" type of play depends upon the needs and objectives relevant to the child and the moment.

Let's look at it this way...

Free Play

Direct Instruction

Sometimes we simply contrast play with direct instruction. Direct instruction is just like it sounds; the teacher gives narrow, specific instruction directly to the passive student who sits quietly and receives it. The *teacher directs* or controls essentially everything in the interaction.

Now, the complete opposite of that would be free play, where the *child directs* the activity completely without any adult support or interaction. That's a pretty stark contrast. If there's nothing in between, it seems the only options are to have children sit perfectly still and listen or to set them loose on their own without any guidance, support, or parameters.

What the spectrum of play clarifies is that it's not just free play "good" and direct instruction "bad." It recognizes that direct instruction is not generally effective, particularly for young learners, but also illustrates that under the banner of Playful Learning, there is a whole range of approaches that are effective, because they respond to the learner's needs and the context of the situation. And all along this spectrum, we honor and maintain the child's sense of agency and joy—core components of play.

Moving along this spectrum, there are shifts in the balance of guidance and direction between the child and the adult in terms of support, materials, supervision, boundaries, and interactions. So, at one end there is more child direction, less adult support, and less of a specific goal or objective, and all along the spectrum, there are varying degrees of those elements. At the far end—beyond the Playful Learning Spectrum—then, there is direct instruction where you find complete adult direction and a very specific and often isolated goal.

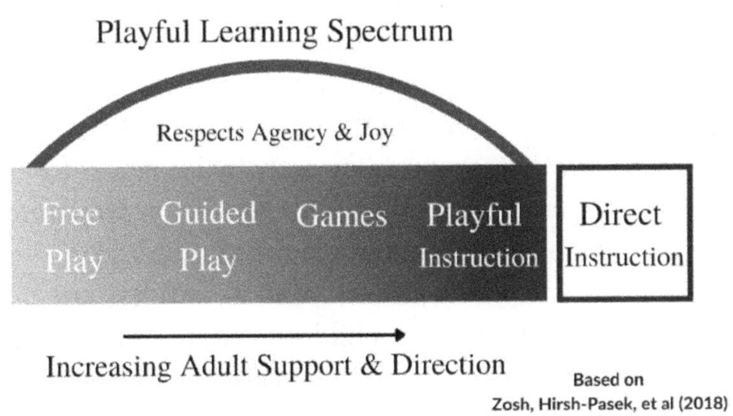

At the free play end of the spectrum, the child initiates and controls the activity with little to no adult involvement and no set goal—yet it still fosters social-emotional growth and development.

But skilled educators don't just set up a play space and step back. Instead, they watch for cues. Does the child seem frustrated? Disengaged? Deeply absorbed? Knowing when to step in and scaffold a child's play versus when to simply observe is an essential skill. A teacher might notice a child struggling with a puzzle and ask, "What piece do you think fits next?" rather than solving it for them. This subtle guidance keeps the play self-directed while adding gentle support.

That's why the next labeled point is guided play. In guided play children still have a great deal of agency and self-direction. It may even *look* or *feel* like free play, but there is a little more support from adults in the way the environment has been prepared with inviting materials and in the way the adults support the play with interactions and conversations. In fact, what is often referred to as free play in a preschool classroom may actually be closer to guided play in this context. If the room has been prepared with specific supplies, if activities are organized to create invitations or provocations, and if adults are having conversations with the children about their play—all elements of a high-quality classroom—that's adding elements of guided play.

Guided play is a sweet spot where we balance engagement and intention without taking over. There's still lots of agency and joy in the child's sphere, but we skillfully support and guide in an individually responsive, thoughtful way. Guided play is where we see a lot of research for fantastic learning outcomes for young children.[5] When we recognize that a large portion of the work we do falls near this guided play range, we can be more intentional about how we support that play.

Other areas on the playful learning range of the spectrum include games. A child may engage in a game that requires some support or teaching from an adult. That would be further to the right in that zone. That balance shifts a bit as the child becomes more proficient and can initiate or even direct the game without help, moving that activity a little further to the left in that zone—more child direction and less adult influence.

Even playful instruction has a place on this spectrum. That may look a bit more like direct instruction—the teacher has more control and a more specific objective in mind—but with a joyful, engaging approach, where the child's agency is still supported. We see this in short snippets of instruction in the classroom—teaching a concept through a song or story—or in play-based therapies where targeted skills are practiced through playful activities.

Let's look at these different types of play experiences in the early childhood classroom. Free play may be represented by a child playing in the block area. It's completely open-ended. No prompting or guidance. In guided play, a teacher may notice a child is interested in how things roll, so she adds ramps and balls to the block area to complement this interest and invite some discovery. She may ask the children playing there questions like, "What happened when you put more blocks under one end of the ramp?" Or, "Which ramp made the ball roll the farthest?" She's gently guiding and supporting the play. Playful learning in a game is pretty easy to recognize—a teacher may help organize a group of children to play a matching game or to feed rhyming words to a puppet, or the children may organize it themselves after learning the rules. And playful instruction could be illustrated by a pre-K teacher using a song to demonstrate and practice rhyming sounds.

There are many different contexts, objectives, and needs throughout the preschool day, and that requires a variety of ways to play. That's how it should be! We're building balanced, whole children with a variety of needs—of course we're going to need to be able to respond in a variety of ways!

It's important to underscore that there is not one type of play that is morally superior to the others. The whole concept of a spectrum does away with the all-or-nothing argument and introduces balance. Preschool children need opportunities to engage in all kinds of play with various amounts of support from adults and from their peers.

I also want to emphasize that while I outlined specific points on this spectrum, moving from one to the other is very fluid. Trying to pinpoint the exact spot where free play becomes guided play is a little like trying to define the precise moment when one shade of blue becomes the next.

The shift happens in gradual degrees, but those shifts are necessary in order to respond to the needs of the child.

Think of it this way: Free play is a powerful driver of social, emotional, and cognitive growth. It's amazing, and all children should get lots of it daily. Likewise, in a dietary sense, blueberries are a superfood, full of important vitamins and fiber. But no matter how awesome blueberries are, if they are the *only* food you eat, you won't be healthy. Because your diet is unbalanced. There's a wide variety of foods you need in your diet to make sure you get well-rounded nutrition and meet your health objectives.

Just like a healthy diet includes more than one superfood, a balanced learning environment includes more than one type of play. Free play is essential, but so are guided play, games, and playful instruction. The key isn't consistently choosing one over the other—it's recognizing what children need to be properly supported. It's a delicate balance that depends on the needs of the children right in front of you.

All types of playful learning have value. The key is knowing when to step back and observe, when to adjust materials, when to engage alongside children, and when to introduce a game or brief playful instruction. Above all, remember: Play exists on a spectrum. Your role is to find the right balance—observing, adapting, and responding to the children's needs in the moment.

Key Takeaways:

- Play is difficult to define because it exists on a **spectrum** and is experienced differently by each child.
- Two essential elements of play are **agency** (self-direction) and **joy** (satisfaction and engagement).
- Research supports a **balanced approach to play**, incorporating free play, guided play, games, and playful instruction.

Reflect:

- **How** does the spectrum of play help us understand different types of play experiences?
- **Reflect** on your own teaching or parenting—are there opportunities to increase guided play without diminishing child-led exploration?

Take Action:

- **Observe** children at play and identify how **agency** and **joy** are present in their experiences.
- **Identify** examples of each type of play on the Spectrum of Playful Learning. Reflect on how to **offer a balance** of playful learning experiences.

CHAPTER 4

Why We Play: Mental Health and Wellness

In 2018, the American Academy of Pediatrics published a clinical report with the title "The Power of Play: A Pediatric Role in Enhancing Development in Young Children."[1] In its preface, the authors said they compiled the report to give pediatricians the information they need to not only promote play, but to literally write a prescription for play.

Let that sink in for a moment.

In a supercharged, screen-based society, childhood play deficits have become so common, and their impact so profound, that doctors felt the need to prescribe play as a medical treatment.

The report states:

"When play and safe, stable, nurturing relationships are missing in a child's life, toxic stress can disrupt the development of executive function and the learning of prosocial behavior; in the presence of childhood adversity, play becomes even more important. The mutual joy and shared communication and attunement...that parents and children can experience during play regulate the body's stress response."

So, when I say play helps promote mental health and wellness for children, it isn't just a feel-good platitude. This is science. In a playful state, a child's brain chemistry is changed. It's awash with beneficial chemicals that promote wellness and growth, while at the same time, harmful stress hormones are reduced.[2]

Knowing that play influences the body's stress response sheds some light on a report published in the *Journal of Pediatrics* about 5 years later, in 2023.[3] It was authored by three scholars—all brilliant in their own right, but one name in particular stood out to me, and that was psychologist Peter Gray. His career has been a decades-long, in-depth study of the psychological impacts of play.

What Gray and his colleagues noted in this article was that while there has been a great deal of attention on the decline in mental health among children and youth in the past decade or so, research actually suggests that this decline has been going on for about 70 years. Over this time, as general mental health has declined, an increase in psychopathological disorders—specifically anxiety, depression, narcissism, and general feelings of helplessness—has been observed.

What these researchers found interesting was that as they looked at this decades-long increase in psychopathology and mental health challenges, you also see a decrease in play for children over that same period of time.

The authors admitted that there are many factors at play, and that correlation does not always indicate causation, but after digging into years of research, they ultimately came to this conclusion: "Our thesis is that a primary cause of the rise in mental disorders is a decline over decades in opportunities for children and teens to play, roam, and engage in other activities independent of direct oversight and control by adults."

We may be quick to blame screens and technology (and there's plenty to be concerned about there), but screens aren't the only culprit. Over the decades, play has steadily been replaced by structured, adult-controlled activities. This shift—less child-led play, more external control—has deeply affected children's mental health. Play requires some element of agency or choice. That agency is just one of the reasons why supporting play contributes to overall mental health and wellness for children.

If you take a look at our culture over the last few decades, it's easy to see an increase in what I call *pervasive passivity*. There's a creeping influence in our modern lives that puts us in a more passive, rather than active, position. This is particularly true for young children today who are often treated as passive passengers, being moved through their own lives, rather than as active agents, making their own choices.

Let's look at three examples.

One place we see this pervasive passivity is with the explosion of digital media. For children today, the amount of time in front of screens and the amount of access to content is exponentially higher than it was decades ago. Not all content is created equal, of course, but regardless of the content, one thing we see, increasingly, is young children in front of screens for extended periods of time, catatonically watching videos and swiping through content. And while they *think* they're making choices about the next video or game, those choices are often predetermined by algorithms. The screen is in control, not the child.

On top of that, it's not uncommon to see technology intentionally used to pacify or distract children—often, in order to quite literally make it easier to passively move them about in their own lives. How many times have you seen young children in a shopping cart, a restaurant booth, or a car seat staring at a video on a phone instead of noticing and interacting with the conversations and active world around them? We are too often using the conveniences of technology to put children in a passive rather than active position, cutting them out of the very experiences that drive development.

But screens aren't the only way we limit children's autonomy. Even in their daily routines, they often have little control over their time. Overscheduling is another place that we find this pervasive passivity. When young children are spending a large chunk of their day in activities that are scheduled, organized, and run by adults, those children end up simply moving from one thing to the next on a conveyor belt of adult-directed checkpoints. At each spot, they'll be told what to do and how to do it. Now, I want to be clear that there are great activities and enrichment programs for children, but (1) if there are too many of them and (2) if they are overly structured and governed by adults, then we are putting children in a passive position—which creates a barrier to their development.

Unfortunately, the third place where we see this pervasive passivity is in too many early learning environments, where young children are expected to sit still, be quiet, and passively receive information. This isn't how young children are wired to learn. We'll talk more about this in a later chapter, but the science of learning tells us that the best learning happens when children are active, not passive, and engaged, not distracted into silence and stillness. A well-run early childhood classroom should have a gentle, busy hum of activity and conversation.

These three examples—screen time, overscheduling, and developmentally inappropriate school settings—

illustrate how our culture is becoming pervasively passive, particularly for children. When we consider what we know about agency, and its impact on development and well-being, we have to recognize that this passivity, or this lack of agency, will have detrimental impacts on young children.

Who Has Control?

In human development, as well as in psychology, we frequently use the term "locus of control" to refer to where people believe control is located. For example, a person may believe control for their life is primarily within them—an internal locus of control—or they may believe that control is outside of them—an external locus of control. The difference between internal and external locus of control lies in whether a person believes the control over the things that really impact and drive their life are within their grasp or beyond it. An internal locus of control says, "I didn't do well on the test because I didn't study. That's something I can change next time." An external locus of control says, "I didn't do well on the test because my teacher doesn't like me. So why bother?"

Research (and common sense) tells us that people who develop a stronger internal locus of control are more likely to be proactive in their lives and to make choices in order to improve and actively reach goals.[4] People with a stronger external locus of control are more likely to say, "Why try?" or "It's not MY fault."

Incidentally, an external locus of control—feeling you don't have control over your life—is also connected with feelings of depression and anxiety.[5] That sounds familiar, so let's circle back to the top. Dr. Gray said that as play has decreased, there has been an increase in psychopathology, including specifically, depression and anxiety. Do you see the connection?

As children are allowed less play, they are allowed less agency. With less experience making choices and being active participants in their own lives, there is an increase in feelings of helplessness and an external locus of control, which is connected to depression and anxiety. It is clear that the agency provided by play serves a critical role in our development and well-being.

While reading a journal article synthesizing the research on agency and its impact on healthy development, I was struck by how frequently the word "essential" was used.[6]

"The belief in one's ability to exert control over the environment and to produce desired results is *essential* for an individual's general well-being..."

"The desire for control is an *essential* component of what it means to be human..."

Researchers are very precise in their language choices. They didn't say control and agency are merely "nice" or "important." They didn't say it only applies to some children. They very intentionally chose the word "essential."

So, if control, choice, and agency are in fact essential, does that mean we should just let children do whatever they want?

No.

But there's an ideal context for children to exert healthy, developmentally appropriate control over their environment...and that's play! In play, children make choices. They build imaginary worlds with the friends they choose to let into them. They get to decide how an entire city is built with blocks—and they get to decide to destroy that city if they wish. They choose what kind of masterpiece to create with paint and loose parts, and they get to dictate how a toy car can be buried in a snowstorm and then saved by a magical unicorn. It takes a lot of power to control all that.

Play gives children an appropriate way to feel control and exercise agency, and that is tightly tied to their mental health.

Play, Risk, and Resilience

Research also tells us that the risk involved with play is another mental health benefit. When children see that they can take risks—whether that's the risk of a skinned knee or a toppled block tower—they see that they can fail and come back from failure. That's how resilience and self-efficacy are built.[7] Likewise, therapists point out that adventurous or risky play mimics the exposure therapy used to treat anxiety—to expose yourself to risk and fear, and to experience the reality that you will be ok. In this way, play becomes a natural form of therapy that children participate in over and over for years.[8]

So, again, as we talk about children needing agency and risk, does that mean we let them run the show and dance with danger?

Of course not.

But we do let them play. Play is the perfect context where they not only get to exercise choice over what to play and who to play with, but in their creative imaginings, they control entire worlds. Play is the perfect place to practice calculating and taking reasonable risks—one more block that might topple the tower, an idea that might be rejected by playmates, even a leap from the swings that might require a band aid. As children take risks, they build self-efficacy when they succeed, and resilience when they fail and move forward anyway. All of these experiences are key to a child's mental health.

Psychologists and physicians are recognizing that there is something about play that is core to our development as humans, and that a severe restriction of play is having negative impacts on many fronts, not least of which is our overall mental health. That mental health undergirds *everything* else. That's why it's first on my list.

We've covered three reasons why play supports mental health and wellness.

1. Play impacts brain chemistry and helps us deal with stress.

2. Play allows children appropriate agency.

3. Play builds resilience through healthy challenges.

There are piles of intricately worded research on this topic, full of charts and graphs and technical terminology. But Dr. Peter Gray sums up the whole body of research quite simply, saying:

"Social play makes children happy, and its absence makes them unhappy."[9]

You don't need a PhD to see the problem: Take away play—a healthy source of agency and a natural reliever of stress and anxiety—and children will struggle and become more vulnerable to mental health challenges. We want more for children. That's why we play for mental health and wellness.

Key Takeaways:

- Research suggests a strong link between **reduced play opportunities** and **increased mental health challenges** in children.
- Play provides **agency, autonomy, and controlled risk-taking**, all of which contribute to emotional well-being.

Reflect:

- **How** does play act as a natural stress reliever for children? How do **you** use play to relieve stress?
- **How** can adults incorporate more opportunities for agency and risk-taking in play while still maintaining necessary levels of safety?

Take Action:

- **Find** opportunities for increasing child-led, unstructured play in your classroom or home environment.
- **Show your support** for recess, outdoor play, and open-ended learning experiences in your local schools and communities.

CHAPTER 5

Why We Play: Brain Development & Deep Learning

Imagine two early childhood classrooms. In one, students sit at desks, tracing letters on worksheets. In the other, children are building forts, making up stories, and negotiating who gets to be the pirate. It might seem like the first group is learning more, but research tells a different story. Landmark studies like the Perry Preschool and Carolina Abecedarian projects show that deep learning—the kind that lasts for a lifetime—happens in school contexts that emphasize language, relationships, family support, and playful learning. Yet today, many programs try to replicate the success of these studies by focusing on the wrong things: structured lessons, assessments, and early academics, missing the deeper forces at work.

Lessons from Landmark Studies

I like to say that everyone has heard of the Perry Preschool and Abecedarian projects, even if they think they haven't. They're among the most cited studies in early childhood education, so even if you're unfamiliar with their names, you've likely encountered their influence—in footnotes of policy discussions, funding proposals, and educational books. (Including this one.[1])

Essentially, research showed that children in these high-quality early childhood programs implemented back in the 1960s and 1970s had positive outcomes that lasted decades. These children excelled beyond their peers on measures related to educational attainment and positive behavior and even showed a ripple effect benefiting subsequent generations long after the initial study.[2]

While nearly every proposal for funding an early childhood education program will cite research from the "gold standard" programs of the 1960s and 1970s—Perry Preschool and Abecedarian—few are replicating their results today.

On top of that, some programs that do show promising improvements on test scores as their children enter kindergarten watch those impacts fade out over the next year or two.

So why aren't modern programs replicating these results? Well, as I mentioned in the introductory chapter, a group of researchers put together a paper in 2023 to explore that exact question.[3] They pointed out that there are many factors to consider when looking at what appears to be a diminishing impact of preschool. Some of it was actually good news—all children were faring a little bit better on certain measures, making the contrast between children in and out of preschool a little less stark.

That's great.

But their other observation is one we all need to pay attention to.

The panel suggested that the decline in program impact was due to a shift in content and methods of modern pre-K programs. While those earlier programs like Perry and Abecedarian implemented developmentally responsive, whole-child, play-based curricula, research shows today's programs are more likely to be influenced by an academic push-down effect. And that push-down often pushes play out.

Essentially, these programs have said, "We want the outcomes of the Perry Preschool Project, but we're not going to do what they did. It's still *called* preschool, so it should be fine."

That's like saying, "I want to make a chocolate cake, but I'm not going to add any chocolate. I'll still call it chocolate cake, and it'll probably taste the same."

It's not enough to simply *say* we have high-quality preschools. The ingredients matter.

So, this finding, that content and methods have shifted in modern preschools, is really important. They're saying that we've changed the main ingredients. We've changed what we teach and how we teach it.

Primarily, the content has begun to overemphasize academic skills, and the methods have become increasingly focused on direct instruction (things like lectures, worksheets, and drills).

The Iceberg Model of Early Learning

To illustrate this trend, Dr. Dale Farran (who led the Tennessee pre-K study discussed in the opening chapter) has proposed an "Iceberg Model of Early Developmental Competencies."[4] The tip of the iceberg—the part we see above water—contains concrete skills like identifying letters, shapes, and numbers. These are sometimes called "constrained skills." The word constrained means restricted or closed, so we're going to think of those as checkbox skills. The box is constrained by its borders, just like the skill is constrained by whether or not it can be done. Yes or no. We check the box. We can easily count the letters a child identifies and check boxes every time a child counts a group of objects. These skills tend to be lumped together as "school readiness skills," and we print them out on checklists and screening assessments. All of that *can* be very useful.

However, Dr. Farran suggests that while these tip-of-the-iceberg skills are important, valuable skills, this collection of checkbox skills is not the objective in and of itself. These skills were also meant to serve as an indicator. She says children showing those indicator skills generally had built them on top of what she refers to as "unconstrained skills"—or more open-ended skills. This includes things that are harder to test and check the box. Things like vocabulary, curiosity, persistence, self-control, and critical thinking.

Those open skills often continue developing over a lifetime and are hard to test and check off as done, but they are absolutely crucial.

Farran suggests that in the past, we could test for those constrained, easy-to-measure skills and trust that they were present because they were built upon the deeper iceberg of unconstrained skills beneath the surface. Unfortunately, what she's observing now is that too many programs are skipping straight to the tip of the iceberg skills as though those were the end goal, rather than the indicators.

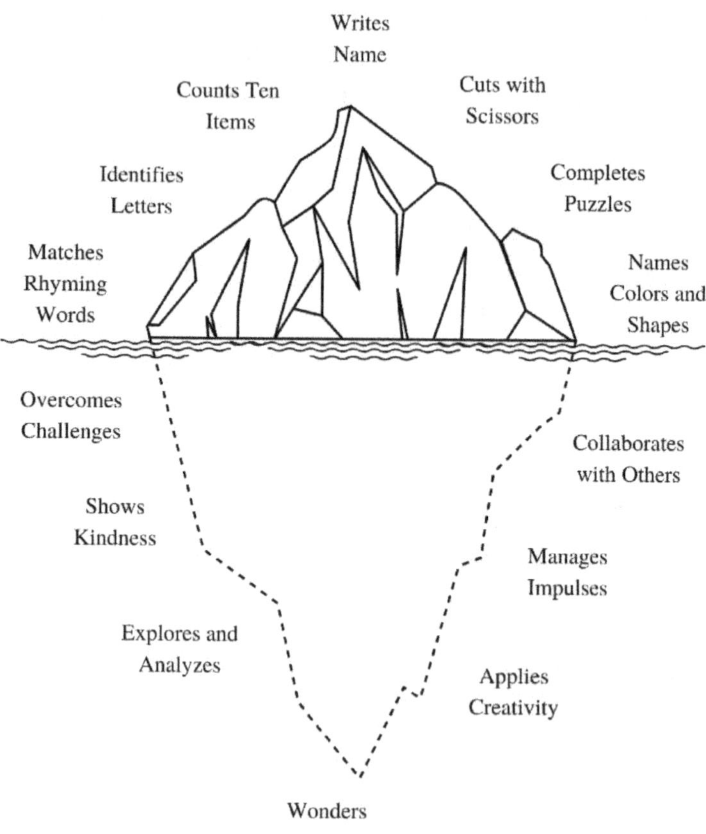

Based on Farran (2022)

A 2021 article in the journal *Child Development*, supports this theory, highlighting that while both constrained and unconstrained skills are important in early childhood programs, constrained skills—those that can be easily measured and checked off—were often taught in isolation and consumed too much instructional time.[5] It's this mismatch, they suggest, that leads to many early pre-K benefits fading out so soon.

Essentially, these programs were "teaching to the test." Or, as Dr. Farran's model suggests, they were building only the tip of the iceberg, neglecting the foundational learning beneath. Because constrained skills are straightforward to teach and assess, and because of the increasing academic pressures in early childhood education, their perceived importance is often overemphasized, leading to an imbalance in instructional priorities. Priorities that cultivate shallow learning.

It makes sense that this shift in focus would then lead to a shift in methods. Emphasizing direct skills often leads to teaching more directly. Research has shown that preschool and pre-K teachers in these modern environments were increasingly likely to use direct instruction—talking *at* the children, rather than *with* them.[6] Ironically, these "direct" methods, and their effort to cut to the chase and get more "directly" at the objectives, are usually less effective in the long run, especially for our youngest learners. It's like killing the goose to get right to the golden egg. And then realizing you have no more golden eggs.

That's because direct instruction often sidesteps other important experiences that research tells us young children need in order to learn and develop—hands-on exploration, social interactions, back and forth conversations, and creative problem-solving. These experiences build that foundation of open, unconstrained skills, which makes it easier for our young learners to build those constrained skills as well.

To be clear, this isn't to say that reading and math skills should be abandoned. But *context* and *focus* matter. Pushing down outsized academic content and methods inevitably pushes out what children actually need. Play. If we're focused on building deep, lasting skills and development, we need to use the right ingredients and in the right proportions.

It isn't enough to simply establish programs for programs' sake. We have to create good ones for the children's sake.

Research tells us that play is an important component of quality programs that build both the checkbox skills and the open skills. And those are the programs that have lasting, long-term results.[7]

High quality early learning programs are language-rich, active, playful, social, and filled with wonder. In that playful environment, academic skills are still built, but they're built better and stronger on a broader, deeper base of skills.

Play and the Brain

That compound effect is one reason why play builds real learning and development. There's also the change in brain chemistry. Beyond shaping essential skills, play has profound effects at the neurological level, literally promoting brain development and learning.

Neuroscientist Dr. Jaak Panksepp was known as "the rat tickler" due to his playful rodent-based studies—one of which literally included tickling rats. In addition to earning a really cool nickname, Panksepp discovered something remarkable: Play activates the brain's learning center. When rats played, their whole neocortex—the area activated for thinking, learning, and remembering—lit up.

Panksepp's studies also showed that after engaging in only 30 minutes of play, rats' brains had more brain-derived neurotrophic factor (or BDNF), a chemical responsible for brain growth and healthy neural connections, than did rats who had not engaged in play.[8] His findings suggest that play isn't just fun; it primes the brain for learning and growth.

That's probably why Dr. Stuart Brown calls play "fertilizer" for the brain.[9] It literally changes the brain's chemistry to promote more brain growth and connection.

Now, clearly, children aren't rats, but there are similarities in the brain structures that allow us to learn from these studies (without crossing some pretty important ethical lines).

While Dr. Brown teaches that play is fertilizer for brain growth, neuroscientist-turned classroom-teacher, Dr. Judy Willis, points out that the reverse is also true. Too much stress or even boredom depresses learning, interrupting the brain from processing new information. In one of my favorite quotes of all time, she shares:

"Neuroimaging research reveals the disturbances in the brain's learning circuits and neurotransmitters that accompany stressful learning environments... Joy and enthusiasm are absolutely essential for learning to happen—literally, scientifically, as a matter of fact and research."[10]

The brain is changed by stress—you've probably experienced that yourself. Think of a time when you were so stressed, so overwhelmed, that you couldn't even process what someone was saying or comprehend something you'd read. I know I've had that happen! I once ended up at the airport hours and hours early because I was so stressed about catching the flight that when I received a notice about a departure change, I completely misread it. Later, in a calm state (probably sometime in the four hours I had to sit around at my gate, waiting for my actual flight), I read the message again and it made perfect sense. But in a stressed-out state, I just couldn't process it properly. It's likely you've had something similar happen. Stress changes brain function and makes it harder to learn and perform.[11]

That happens to our children as well. When their learning environment is overly stressful, when it doesn't respond to the needs of their growing, developing young brains, those brains can no longer respond optimally. In this state, the child's own brain chemistry interferes with information being processed properly.

My favorite part, however, is the other side of that. We don't need joyful, enthusiastic, playful learning environments because they're cute or because we're nice humans (though being a nice human is always strongly encouraged). We build playful learning environments because joy and enthusiasm are "literally, scientifically, as a matter of fact and research"..."essential for learning to happen." We play because it allows brains to learn effectively.

I don't have the access to the brain scanners or the rats to test this out with you the way scientists do in the lab, but let's try it this way. When you finish this chapter, find someone to talk with about how you both played as children. Really dig into the memories, and have them do the same. Don't just say, "I guess I played outside." What did you play? Who were you with? How long did you play? What did it sound like or smell like? Really get deep into the details.

Now, pay attention to your partner. What happens to their face? Their eyes? Their body language? What shifts do you feel in your own body as you reminisce?

I love doing this in person with big groups, because something happens as they talk to one another about their play memories. People's eyes light up! They smile and laugh. Their faces beam, and in a room full of people engaging in this exercise, the whole room changes and the energy shifts.

That's an outward representation of what play does inside the brain. Your eyes and your face light up, and your brain lights up too. Play literally changes our brain chemistry and prepares us for learning.

Play and Curiosity

Play also goes hand in hand with wonder and curiosity—play is really the scientific method in action. Children ask questions or wonder about something. "What happens if I mix the playdough?" Or, "I wonder if I could dig to the bottom of the sandbox." Or, "How could I play the mom in this dress-up scenario?" Then children play with that idea—or in adult terms, they make and test hypotheses. And in their own way, they share and analyze those results and use that information for their next scientific endeavor. Curiosity drives play, and it drives real, authentic learning. The kind of learning that lasts a lifetime.

Back in 2018, a longitudinal study done by researchers at the University of Michigan looked at over 6,000 children as infants, toddlers, preschoolers, and into their kindergarten years.[12] What they were looking for was what kind of effect the children's curiosity had on their academic levels (measured by reading and math scores) in kindergarten. Now, you may not be surprised to know that curiosity was definitely positively related to academic performance, meaning that the most curious babies, toddlers, and preschoolers became the kindergarteners who demonstrated the most academic knowledge when tested. It makes sense that children who ask more questions, would learn more about lots of things.

But one important finding was a bit more surprising. This connection between curiosity and academics was even more pronounced for children from low SES, or socio-economic status. This is a significant detail, since the "achievement gap" between advantaged and disadvantaged students is a critical challenge in education.

Part of the challenge is that for many children (and disproportionately for disadvantaged children), their early learning environments are often more focused on teaching them to sit still and be quiet than on encouraging them to wonder and think out loud. That active, playful, curiosity-driven learning can sometimes be noisy and busy. But based on the information in their study, these researchers drew the conclusion that curiosity—perhaps even more than rigid, studious behavior—is key to learning. They suggested we put less emphasis on getting kids to sit still and more emphasis on keeping them curious.

An article in *The Guardian*, quoted the lead researcher in this study, Dr. Prachi Shah, as saying, "Promoting curiosity in children, especially those from environments of economic disadvantage, may be an important, under-recognized way to address the achievement gap. Promoting curiosity is a foundation for early learning that we should be emphasizing more when we look at academic achievement."[13]

Similarly, a study several years earlier, observed preschool-aged children with their parents and found that in their sample, those children averaged over 100 questions an HOUR.[14] (That means early childhood teachers probably field tens of thousands every day, right?) Young children are naturally very curious!

Unfortunately, subsequent research showed that children just a bit older than the previous sample—the youngest students in elementary school—asked only about 1 or 2 questions per hour.[15] And by fifth grade there were hours-long stretches where children didn't ask any questions at all. This decline parallels the shift away from play-based learning, as structured instruction often leaves little room for exploration and inquiry. It doesn't just reflect a developmental progression; it mirrors a drop in school engagement. When curiosity fades, so does deep learning.

Young children are wired for curiosity, and they are wired for play. It's a self-reinforcing system. This design drives their development and learning. That's why, when people ask if the best early learning programs should focus on learning or play, I'm quick to point out that that is a false dichotomy. It isn't an either/or situation where either we can play or we can learn. It isn't even that we play for certain parts of the day and we learn in other parts of the day. We play *SO* that we can learn.

Play is the method. Learning is the outcome.

Write it down, put it on your wall, write it on your arm if you have to.

Play is the *method.* Learning is the *outcome.*

We have to get really clear on that. It isn't one or the other. Play is the tool that we use, because it is the best way to support the desired outcome of meaningful learning.

So, why does play matter so much? Well, when it comes to learning and brain development, the research reveals three key reasons:

1. Play supports both constrained, checkbox skills *and* open, unconstrained skills. This leads to long term results and less fadeout.

2. Play changes the brain chemistry to promote learning and growth.

3. Curiosity drives both play and meaningful learning. (That's why play is the method and learning is the outcome.)

There are stacks of research to support the effectiveness of play as a driver of development and learning. But perhaps some of the best research you have access to is the learning you get to witness right in front of you. Take a moment to observe children at play. Listen to their questions. Watch how they solve problems. Instead of asking, "Why are they just playing?" ask, "What are they learning through play?" When we recognize play as a powerful driver of learning and development, we start seeing the everyday magic happening right in front of us—and that realization changes everything.

Key Takeaways:

- Landmark studies like **Perry Preschool** and **Abecedarian** show the long-term benefits of high-quality, play-based early education.
- Modern preschool programs often emphasize **constrained** (checkbox) skills at the expense of **unconstrained** (open-ended) skills—leading to short-lived outcomes.
- **Play** activates brain development, promotes learning, enhances memory, and fosters creativity.

Reflect:

- **How** does play support both constrained and unconstrained skill development?
- **How** can educators incorporate more play-based strategies while still meeting academic standards?

Take Action:

- **Observe** an early childhood setting. Are children given opportunities for curiosity-driven exploration?
- **Discuss** the Iceberg Model with educators and parents. Are we prioritizing deep learning or just surface-level skills?

CHAPTER 6

Why We Play: Soft Skills

In conversations about early childhood education, we often hear about the importance of academics—reading, writing, and arithmetic. But when we look at what truly sets people up for success in school, work, and life, it's not just those checkbox skills. It's something deeper, more adaptable, and harder to measure. It's soft skills.

In the previous chapter, we talked about constrained (checkbox) skills and unconstrained (open-ended) skills. While standardized tests often measure constrained skills, it's the open-ended skills that sustain learning and growth over time. Soft skills are part of this open category, and they're the skills that allow people to not just complete tasks but to innovate, collaborate, and thrive.

Soft skills—like communication, teamwork, critical thinking, and emotional intelligence—are often underestimated because they aren't easy to quantify. Yet, in an age where technology is rapidly taking over rote tasks, these human-centered abilities are more valuable than ever. Employers seek them. Leaders rely on them. Families and communities are strengthened by them. Children need to develop soft skills not just so they can be "employable" in some distant future, but so they can confidently, effectively, and happily move through their entire lives—starting right now.

But here's the key: You can't teach soft skills with a worksheet. You don't develop critical thinking by matching a definition on a test. You don't build communication skills by sitting silently in a lecture or staring at a screen. These skills grow through experience, through interaction, through doing.

And that's where play comes in.

Play naturally challenges children to collaborate, solve problems, take risks, and build resilience. It creates real-world scenarios where they practice negotiating, leading, adapting, and empathizing—all without a scripted lesson plan.

In this chapter, we'll explore some of the most essential soft skills and how play lays the foundation for them. Through research and real-world examples, we'll see why fostering these skills in early childhood isn't just a bonus—it's essential for long-term success.

Hard Skills vs. Soft Skills—What's the Difference?

Before we dive into a few pieces of research that show us how play supports these critical soft skills, let's clarify what is meant by "hard skills" and "soft skills." In a general sense, hard skills are required to successfully do a finite task, while soft skills are required for life's infinite range of human challenges.

More specifically, hard skills enable a surgeon to perform a successful appendectomy. While soft skills enable that same surgeon to get along with coworkers, communicate with the patient and family pre- and post-surgery, and quite frankly, avoid losing a medical license for ethics violations. Any professional—any human—can be proficient in hard skills and still struggle immensely due to a lack of soft skills.

There's no definitive catalog of soft skills out there, but drawing from a wide array of lists, here are several common examples:

Communication, Teamwork, Creativity, Planning, Organization, Attention to Detail, Conflict Management, Leadership, Problem-Solving, Curiosity, Flexibility, Critical Thinking, Emotional Intelligence, Social Skills, Empathy, Decisiveness, Perseverance.

If you took the time to observe a group of young children in a preschool or pre-K classroom with this list in mind (and I highly recommend you do), where would you expect to see these skills on display? You'd see them as children build towers with their friends in the block area, as they negotiate roles and set the scene for playing house in the dramatic play area, and as they share materials and ideas at the art table. Play presents children with challenges and opportunities that are ideal for developing these skills.

Play as a Training Ground for Soft Skills

If you're like me, you love to see the science right in front of your eyes, but you also want to see the science in the literature as well. (Or you have a parent or administrator who does.) Don't worry. I've got you. Let's start with persistence and problem-solving.

In a recent study, researchers presented children with a novel game they'd never played before.[1] They then let the children make choices about how the game was modified—changes that would make the game more or less challenging to play. In one group, the children were playing for points and prizes. In the other group, children were simply playing for fun.

What researchers discovered was that when children were playing for points and prizes, they adapted the game to make it easier. They wanted the safe bet. But when they were playing for fun, children consistently made the game more challenging. There's something inherently satisfying about taking on a challenge and overcoming it. That's also part of play! If we want children to develop soft skills like persistence, problem-solving, and resilience, we don't need to put them into learning situations with higher and higher stakes. If we give them opportunities to play, they will naturally look for *just right* challenges that will stretch their abilities!

Play doesn't just build inward-facing soft skills like persistence and problem-solving—it also fosters the kinds of outward-facing soft skills that shape long-term success. Let's look at the soft skills that are often lumped together as social skills.

In a study begun back in the 1990s, researchers looked at a sample of kindergarten children from four different locations in the US and with various risk factors.[2] They had teacher-reported assessments of each child on the following skills:

Peer Problem Solving, Understanding People's Feelings, Shares Materials with Others, Cooperates with Peers, Is Helpful to Others, Listens to Others' Point of View, Can Share Ideas/Opinions Tactfully, Is Friendly.

(I don't know about you, but I noticed several things on that list that would benefit all of us if more adults worked on those skills too!)

After teachers had evaluated these kindergarteners on this list of social skills, researchers checked in on them TWO DECADES later to see if there was any correlation between their long-term outcomes and the measured social skills.

What they found was that children who had been rated as having higher social skills as kindergarteners were statistically significantly more likely to graduate from high school on time, go to college, and be employed. They were also less likely to be arrested, use public assistance, or show substance abuse behaviors. Those are big life outcomes. And they weren't predicted by who learned to read first or who scored highest on the standardized test in the third grade. They were connected to social skills. Social skills that are built, not by flashcards and lectures, but as children interact with other children in play, and when they're guided and supported by adults who know how important these skills are.

The Long-Term Cost of Neglecting Soft Skills

Unfortunately, there's evidence that suggests early school environments have been moving away from these play-based practices, and children are paying the price. About 20 years ago, Dr. Walter Gilliam, a researcher from Yale University, released a study examining the expulsion rates of preschoolers from public programs.[3] That's right—expulsion. As in kicked out. Dr. Gilliam found that in his large, nationally representative sample of prekindergarten programs, preschoolers were being expelled at THREE TIMES the rate of students in grades K-12.[4]

Are preschoolers really three times as difficult as their older counterparts? That seems unlikely.

Gilliam outlined several factors that contribute to this elevated rate of expulsions. All deserve our consideration as we create quality early childhood programs, but two in particular catch my attention.

The first is dramatic play. You may remember it from your own preschool experience. You and your friends dress up and play house, launch into outer space, or save the world. Maybe even all three in one afternoon. In Dr. Gilliam's research, he found that preschool programs offering dramatic play every day had an expulsion rate of 9.4%, while programs that reported offering dramatic play "once a month or never" saw a much-elevated rate of 25.5%.[5] Similarly, programs that reported using worksheets and flashcards daily reported higher expulsion rates than those that used them rarely or never.

It seems that in a developmentally appropriate, play-based approach to early education, children have the opportunity to practice and build soft skills. In inappropriate environments, they're punished for not already having them.

Now, put that data to the side for a moment, and let's look at another study.

A paper out of the Curry School of Education at the University of Virginia examined the question, "Is Kindergarten the New First Grade?"[6] In it, researchers Bassok, Latham, and Rorem compared responses about attitudes and practices of a large, national sample of early childhood teachers between 1998 and 2010. While there were many startling shifts highlighted by their comparison, two findings stood out, particularly when set side by side with Gilliam's research noted above.

As kindergarten teachers responded to questions about the availability of specific areas or centers for activity in their room, there was an obvious shift when it came to the dramatic play area. In 1998, 87% of respondents reported having a dramatic play area in their kindergarten room. In 2010, that number dropped to 58%. That's almost a 30% decrease over those 12 years.

At the same time, teachers reported a 15% increase in math worksheet use and a 16% increase in reading worksheet use.

So, let's summarize these two studies.[7] Here's what we know, based on research:

- Children are more likely to be expelled from programs that use **more** worksheets and **less** dramatic play. (Gilliam)

- The trend is for programs to **increase** their use of worksheets and **decrease** their use of dramatic play. (Bassok, Latham, Rorem)

Notice a problem here? The pattern emerging from these studies is concerning: As early education programs shift away from play and soft skill development, children are facing higher expulsion rates and fewer opportunities to build the skills they seem to lack—skills that truly matter.

But what happens when we take a step back and look at the long-term impact of early education approaches?

That's exactly what researchers did in a study of the Universal Preschool Program in Boston, and their findings offer an important and hopeful contrast to the troubling trends we've just explored.

From Fadeout Effect to Sleeper Effect

Early on, Boston's program seemed to show mediocre results.[8] In elementary and middle school, the participants didn't have substantially higher academic test scores than the children who weren't in the program. It seemed to be a classic case of fadeout. But as researchers continued to follow the children, they began to notice some statistically significant differences in the long-term. The children who participated in the preschool program, which had a strong focus on soft skills and play-based learning, were more likely to graduate high school, take the SAT, and go to college. And they were less likely to be suspended or incarcerated.

These long-term positive outcomes after lackluster early academic outcomes have been referred to as the "Sleeper Effect." They contrast sharply with the "Fadeout Effect" commonly seen in other programs that overemphasize early academic skills but end up with few long-term benefits (or even negative ones as in the Tennessee example from the opening chapter).

In responding to this research, one of my favorite developmental psychologists, Dr. Allison Gopnik, said this:

"Maybe 'preschool' is a misnomer—the programs don't work because they teach specific *school* skills. Instead, the crucial ingredients may be caring adults and a chance to play—fundamental parts of good early childhood programs, large or small, private or public..."

"...Other research suggests that *care* and *play* don't make you better at doing any one particular thing. Instead, they make you more robust and resilient, better able to deal with the unexpected twists and turns of fate. And, ultimately, that may be the best path to success."[9]

What she's saying is that maybe it's the soft skills that are most important. That through play, children develop the skills that apply to all kinds of situations—flexible, soft skills. And that those are the skills that last.

When I see multiple studies like these saying there's a fadeout effect for push-down academic skills, but that there are consistent long-term effects for soft skills, I have to conclude that opportunities for these soft skills are **essential** to early childhood development.

And as Dr. Gopnik and many others have said, those skills are best built by play.

Hopefully by now, you're seeing how all these pieces are interconnected:

1. As children play with calculated risk, agency, and autonomy, they not only support their mental

health, they also build the soft skills of resilience, problem-solving, and confidence.

2. As we use play to support soft skills like critical thinking and communication, we also support academic skills in a sustainable, meaningful way.

This is part of why I say play is powerful. It effectively supports so many meaningful objectives all at once! If we truly want to equip children for lifelong success, we must ensure that play remains at the heart of early childhood education.

Key Takeaways:

- **Soft skills** are critical for success in school, work, and life.
- Play provides **real-world practice** for developing these skills in a natural, engaging way.
- Research shows that **early social competence** strongly predicts future educational and career success.

Reflect:

- **Consider** examples from your own experiences/observations. What happens when a person has high academic skills but lacks soft skills?
- **What** strategies do you use to support soft skill practice?

Take Action:

- **Observe** a group of children at play. What soft skills are they demonstrating?
- **Evaluate** your curriculum. Are there enough opportunities for social skill development?
- **Share** a research-based insight on soft skills and play with a parent, educator, or administrator.

CHAPTER 7

Why We Play: Because We're Human

For years, I've shared three reasons why children need play in early learning environments:

- It's crucial for helping them to secure mental health and wellness.
- It's necessary for brain development and real learning.
- And it's the ideal context for practicing critical soft skills.

But I'm going to add a fourth one here because it's so important, and honestly, I'm a little embarrassed I didn't include it sooner.

Play is the perfect way for children to build human relationships, which is a key driver of healthy development.

Whether we're talking about play between children, or between adults and children, or even play between children and imaginary characters, children are so often playing with and within human relationships.

My favorite precept from decades of studying human development is this:

All human development happens in the context of human relationships.

This simple strand of truth is woven through all kinds of research on human development and human behavior. Development is driven and supported by our interactions with other humans.

We've seen painful evidence of what happens when the physical needs of young children are met, but the relationships are missing. A heartbreaking example of this comes from the Romanian orphanages of the 1990s. Reports and videos revealed children who had been fed and kept alive but were deprived of human interaction. The result? Many suffered severe developmental delays or even death. Our human development happens in the context of human relationships.

Wired to Learn: The Human Edge

Psychologist, Dr. Allison Gopnik, has an interesting perspective on this truth about human development. Because Dr. Gopnik specializes in human development and learning, she's been contacted by some interesting research partners—AI developers. These researchers have reached out to her because despite all the advancements in technology, AI is still not as effective at learning as a human baby.

Isn't it ironic that in an age when we have scientists trying to teach computers to learn more like children, we would have systems and programs trying to get children to learn more like computers—as though you could just squish information in and churn information out?

But that's not how humans learn. Humans learn in the context of human relationships. Dr. Gopnik says this:

"(A) crucial factor that sets children apart from AIs is the way that they learn *socially*, from other people. AIs can learn from very specific and *controlled* kinds of human supervision. But human children learn from the people around them in much more *sophisticated* ways."

"Another secret of children's learning...they are insatiably *curious* and *active* experimenters... AIs have mostly been stuck inside their mainframes *passively* absorbing data... We're collaborating with computer scientists...who try to make AIs that are similarly *curious*, *active* learners."[1]

Children aren't data processors; they are social learners, wired to grow through relationships.

I hope you're recognizing elements of what we've explored in previous chapters. Children learn best when they are active, have agency, and are allowed to be curious. Children learn best as they play. But the other important element is that they do all this in the context of social relationships. They learn from their interactions (both with adults and with other children) and in a way that is more powerful than the most sophisticated piece of technology.

Interaction, Not Just Supervision

So, what's going on in these social interactions? Well, one fascinating piece of research from Princeton University's Baby Lab gives us an idea.[2] In a unique experiment, researchers brought toddlers in to interact with researchers in really simple play-based situations. They would play with toys together, sing a song, or read a book. But researchers didn't just watch what was happening on the outside of these interactions. They were mapping what was going on with the brain activity for both the child and the adult in these scenarios. And what they found was remarkable.

First of all, they found that brain activity for the adult and toddler began to sync up. They described the patterns moving in tandem like a beautiful dance. And it wasn't just the adult leading. Sometimes the child's brain activity was leading and the adult's activity followed suit. This observation should remind us that the children are active participants exercising agency in these interactions.

Next, they noticed that a lot of this activity was happening in the prefrontal cortex. That's an advanced part of the brain, and it doesn't finish developing until our early 20s. (If you have teenagers, you've seen this in action—there's a reason their decision-making isn't always stellar. Their brains are literally still under construction in this key area!)

Seeing the prefrontal cortex light up in these toddlers was quite remarkable because generally, we wouldn't expect so much activity in that area in such a young child. These interactions aren't just fun—they're brain-building. When we connect, talk, and play with young children, our more developed brains sync up with theirs. This helps scaffold their development, particularly in advanced areas like the prefrontal cortex. That's powerful! That's part of why children are wired to seek out interactions!

Now, there was one more key piece to this study. Any good study has a control. So, at the end of the interaction, the adult researcher would turn away from the child and talk to another adult in the room. This helped to isolate the variable they were testing. It showed that the brain activity—that beautiful dance—was in response to the adult's interactions with the child, not just to the sound of the adult's voice. When the adult turned and talked to another person in the room, that dance, that interconnection, just...stopped. The brainwaves began moving independently again. That tells me that it's not enough for us to simply supervise play like lifeguards up in a chair. We can't just be in the room and make sure no one runs with scissors or shoves marbles up their noses. We have to engage and interact, and we need to support children as they interact with one another.

In fact, in 2017, the Brookings Institution, a well-respected think tank in the United States, gathered ten leading experts on early education to pool their research and observations in order to answer some important questions, including: "What are the factors that make one pre-K program more effective than another?"[3] There are many "right" answers to this question. Resources matter, ratios matter, but the tricky thing about studying human development is that there are so many variables, it's often hard to answer a question like this with real certainty.

If you read a lot of research in human development, you quickly see how careful and precise researchers are with their words. "*This* factor had *this* effect but *sometimes* it didn't, and given *different conditions* you might see *something else*." And, honestly, that's how some of this panel's answers sounded. That's why one statement really jumped off the page for me. Their report said:

"Developmental science tells us that a key ingredient is the instructional, social, and emotional 'serve-and-return' interactions that occur daily between teachers and children, as well as among classmates."

They didn't say that "sometimes" interactions mattered. They didn't say that only instructional interactions mattered. They said the instructional, social, and emotional interactions between children and between children and teachers were not just important, they were another *key ingredient*. Including them is like adding the rest of the chocolate in the chocolate cake recipe.

No matter how fancy your school's sign is or how good your marketing is, if you say you're a high-quality program and you don't prioritize relationships and interactions, you're not a high-quality program. It doesn't matter what you call it if you're missing a key ingredient.

And where do we find those high-quality child-to-child or child-to-adult interactions? We don't find many as they sit silently on the rug or when they "catch a bubble" before walking down the hallway. We don't see many while they hunch over worksheets or swipe screens on devices. High-quality interactions happen most frequently and most naturally during play.

The best programs don't just *allow* play—they *prioritize* it as a foundation for learning. Play creates the perfect context for children to build and learn within relationships and interactions. It's how we're wired as humans rather than computers. Play is not just cute—it's how children grow, connect, and thrive. It's how they become fully human. And as educators, caregivers, and parents, we have the privilege of fostering that. It's another reason why we play.

Key Takeaways:

- Human development is driven by **relationships and social interactions**.
- Play creates the **ideal context** for building these human connections.
- Research shows that brain activity in children **syncs with adults** during engaged play, fostering cognitive and emotional growth.

Reflect:

- **How** does play strengthen relationships in your early childhood settings as well as in your own life?
- **What** are the differences between passive supervision and active engagement during play?

Take Action:

- **Observe** a play-based interaction. What do you notice about the back-and-forth exchanges? What tools do both sides use to encourage engagement?
- **Create** more opportunities for meaningful "serve-and-return" interactions in your home or school setting.

CHAPTER 8

Powerful Play in Early Education

We've covered crucial reasons why young children need play to support learning and healthy development. But maybe you or someone you know is still saying, "Of course. I *know* play is important. But children get that play at recess or outside of school. Play at school is a waste of time. School is for *learning*."

I've heard this sentiment countless times, and my response to educators and caregivers is always the same: *"Play is the method; learning is the outcome."*

Play and learning are not competing for our time or resources. They are not two separate categories. Rather, they are completely intertwined. Play is the method, the tool we use to support powerful learning. To say we have so much learning to do that we don't have time for play is like saying we have too many miles to drive, so we don't have time to gas up. Play is fuel for learning.

Active Discovery: How Play Unlocks Understanding

Research consistently shows that children learn best through play with *just right* support from responsive adults. This combination creates a powerful catalyst for learning and development.

One such study demonstrates the power of active discovery through play. In this example, preschoolers were shown a new toy that would light up under specific conditions.[1] One group explored the toy first, discovering its features before the experimenter demonstrated how to make it light up. In the second group, the experimenter first showed the children exactly how to get the toy to light and then let them play.

Researchers found children in the first group understood the toy better because they actively explored first, then received guidance. They were primed to make new information meaningful. While both groups used play and adult support, researchers concluded that the way the adult supported the child's process of active discovery was a powerful part of that learning process.

Discovery-based learning played an important role in a subsequent study where the experimenter showed children another novel toy that could respond to different actions with sounds and lights.[2] With one group of children, the researcher demonstrated—or directly taught—one specific way to use the toy and get it to make a squeaking sound. In essence, they said:

"Here's the toy. Here's how it works."

In another group, the researcher invited curiosity by pretending to stumble upon the toy's features, essentially modeling the discovery process in front of the children. It may have sounded something like this:

"Wow, what do you think this toy does? Oh, my goodness! How did it make that sound? Did you hear that? What made that happen? You think it was when I pulled this tube?"

When these two groups of children, who had been introduced to the toy in different ways, were then allowed to play with the toy, the direct instruction group spent more time repeating the function that had been taught to them. They replicated what they had been shown and made the toy squeak. But in the discovery group, the teacher not only modeled how to make the sound, that teacher modeled the *process of discovery*. In that group, when the children were allowed to play with the toy, they continued to explore and found not just one, but *multiple* ways to get the toy to function. They not only made the squeaking sound but also discovered hidden features like making it light up. Here again, children learned best when the process of active discovery was supported and enhanced by an adult who modeled and scaffolded, but didn't take over.

Now this is where it gets really interesting. After establishing active discovery through play as a learning tool, researchers asked what method might be most effective for meeting specific learning objectives.

For this particular study, they decided the targeted objective would be learning about the attributes of a triangle —three sides, three points, three angles.[3] Fittingly, they also had three groups. All three groups had an adult experimenter as the "teacher" and the same hands-on materials—shape cards and manipulatives. There was a free play group, where the children could play with the materials in any way they wanted. There was a direct instruction group where the "teacher" talked about the different parts of a triangle and demonstrated with the materials while the children passively listened and followed instructions. And then there was also a guided play group—a sort of middle of the road—where the "teacher" encouraged and interacted with the children as they explored triangles together.

Researchers found that both the direct instruction and guided play children actually learned more about triangles than the free play group, but the guided play group—with that responsive balance of support—had a deeper knowledge, making it possible for them to identify even the atypical triangles that the direct instruction group often missed. Once again, children learned best with just enough guidance to enhance discovery.

The Power of Guided Play

In writing about these studies in the article "Guided Play: Principles and Practices," a panel of five researchers asserted:

"Such studies remind us that the balance between adult scaffolding and self-direction can and should shift depending on the learners' abilities and the learning goals."[4]

There's no set amount. No prescribed perfection. The balance shifts as we respond to the children in front of us. They go on to say:

"A combination of children's self-directed participation and adult scaffolding creates a powerful pedagogical approach for learning in young children...there is a vast pedagogical space between the stark dichotomy of free play and direct instruction."

Again, we see that Spectrum of Playful Learning introduced in Chapter 3. There is a full range—"a vast pedagogical space"—between free play and direct instruction. Within this range, there is room for responsive support and guidance. This balance—of allowing children to discover and shifting our guidance to support them through the process—is a critical aspect of effective early education. This is why early childhood education can't be scripted or replaced by videos, computer programs, or even AI. It requires us to be present, observant, and adaptable—responding to the cues children give us through their play. Despite the many misconceptions, powerful play isn't an unstructured free-for-all, nor is it rigid, predetermined lessons. Instead, it's about finding the blend of child-driven exploration and thoughtful adult guidance.

I often use the visual of a child on a playground swing to illustrate this balance. Picture a child swinging at the park—laughing, soaring, feeling a rush of air. It looks like pure freedom, like flying.

But if you look closer, that freedom is only possible because of the swing's structure. The seat provides support, and the chains offer guidance. Without them, the child wouldn't be swinging—they'd simply fall.

When we watch a child on a swing, we rarely focus on the structure itself. We only notice it when it's off balance—when the swing is too rigid to move or too loose to be safe. The same is true in a play-based classroom. At first glance, it may look like chaotic, unstructured play. But when you look and listen more closely, you'll see a skillful and intentional balance of structure, support, and guidance. And when it's done really well, it's so seamless it looks like "just playing."

So, how do we strike this balance? What does powerful play in the early childhood classroom look like?

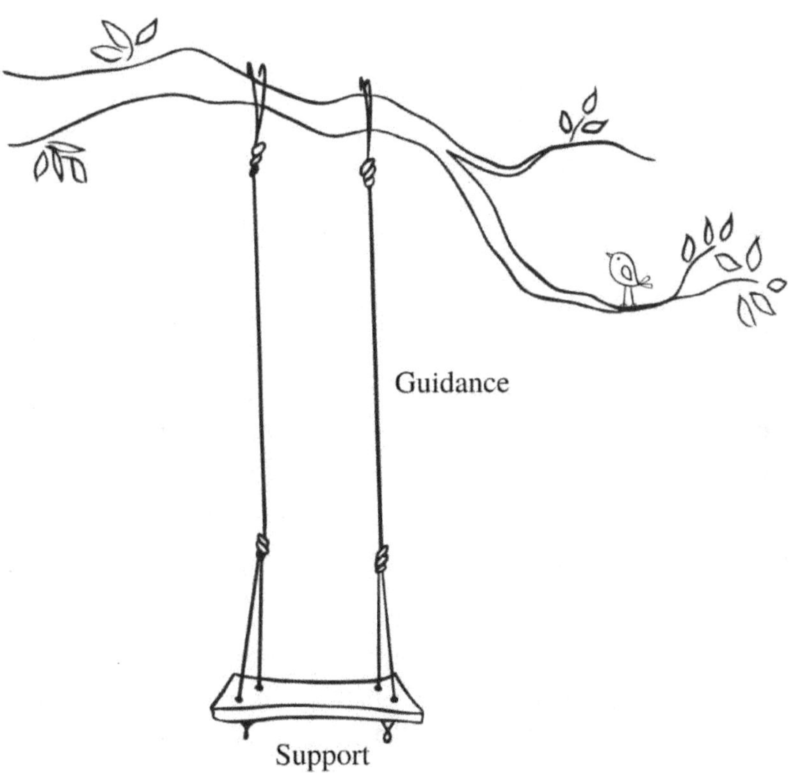
Guidance
Support

Researchers taking a multidisciplinary approach to define the science of learning identified core components of effective learning environments. Building on this, one of those researchers, Dr. Kathy Hirsh Pasek, and her colleagues observed that these same elements also define a playful learning environment.[5] In other words, the science of learning and playful learning are inherently aligned. These powerful learning environments are active, engaging, meaningful, social, joyful, and iterative. Therefore, we want to see playful classrooms with those same elements.

It's no coincidence that these elements are found all along the Spectrum of Playful Learning, discussed previously. This framework emphasizes that adult involvement can vary across a continuum, from free, child-directed play to highly structured, teacher-guided activities. There's no singular "right" way for play to look. Instead, it should be responsive to the children and their developmental needs.

But powerful play is not only responsive—it's also intentional. Some educators may resist the idea that intentionality has a place in play-based learning, fearing it could strip play of its magic. However, intentionality is not about controlling or over-directing play. Rather, it's about understanding the proximal developmental goals and using play as a tool to meet those objectives while preserving the child's agency and joy.

To effectively support this kind of intentional, powerful play, I use a framework in my trainings called the *Recognize*

– *Emphasize – Maximize* method. This approach helps educators identify key aspects of play that can enhance learning and developmental outcomes. Whether you're looking to better understand the process for your own teaching practice or to better recognize it in your observations as a parent or administrator, these are important elements to keep in mind.

Recognize – Emphasize – Maximize

The *Recognize – Emphasize – Maximize* method tells us that when we are intentional about recognizing some key pieces of information, we can use that information to help us emphasize important aspects of each play activity, and by doing so, we maximize the developmental and learning outcomes (and, incidentally, the JOY) for young learners.

Recognize

First, let's break down the *Recognize* step.

There are three aspects we want to make sure to *Recognize* as we support powerful play.

1- The Potential of Play: We've done a lot of this already in this book. Understanding why play is so important for young learners helps us to better recognize the power and potential in the play activities we're supporting.

2- Developmental and Learning Domains: Knowing how children develop in various areas—cognitive, social, emotional, physical—allows us to better support play in a way that helps children grow in every domain.

3- The Needs of the Whole Child: Recognizing the individual child's needs is of paramount importance. This awareness allows us to adapt and respond in ways no scripted lesson or algorithm ever could—because human connection is a dynamic, responsive dance. By observing play, we gather invaluable insights into each child's interests, strengths, and challenges, allowing us to guide and support them in more meaningful, impactful ways.

Emphasize

Once we've recognized these key aspects, the next step is to put that knowledge into action. This is where intentionality comes into play: We emphasize what matters most for each child's development.

I like to focus the *Emphasize* phase on three words starting with I: invitations, implementation, and interactions. We customize and prepare our environment and activities with the right invitations to engage children. We make choices about how to implement those activities—how to adapt and change and put them into action in a way that is *just right* to meet the needs of the children we're working with. And, perhaps most importantly, we use the information to help us know how and when to best interact with the children as they play.

For instance, if we recognize a child needs support in developing fine motor skills in particular, we may emphasize that skill by creating invitations through a variety of tools and appealing activities throughout the classroom, which he can choose to play with to strengthen hands and fingers (playdough, paintbrushes, scissors, lacing beads, small building blocks, digging tools, etc.). We make implementation choices about what we add or remove and how we support that play, based on what we know about this particular child and what we see happening in the moment. (Do we meet him where he's at by swapping pipe cleaners for string with the lacing beads?) And in our interactions, we observe, connect, and support that development.

If we recognize a need to emphasize the soft skill of resilience with another child, we prepare the environment to invite her into enticing activities that have an element of risk (inherent in play—blocks fall down, paint sometimes smudges, puzzles are often puzzling). We're mindful in our implementation, finding *just right* challenges and staying nearby to support and coach her through her frustration. And we ensure that in our interactions we model scripts that are validating and coach her through the problem-solving process.

That may sound like a lot, but it becomes a natural part of a playful environment. Skilled teachers are doing all of that (times 12 or 17 or 20!) all day long. It's a honed skill that allows them to intentionally plan and implement powerful playful learning. When educators bring that intentionality to the classroom, and when parents and administrators recognize that intentionality, children are supported and learn more effectively and more joyfully.

Maximize

By allowing the Recognize phase to influence the Emphasize phase, we're naturally led to Maximize positive outcomes for children. We've recognized that these activities we plan each day aren't just "cute." They aren't just meant to fill up the day or keep children busy. These play experiences that have been intentionally chosen, prepared, and supported are powerful drivers of learning and development.

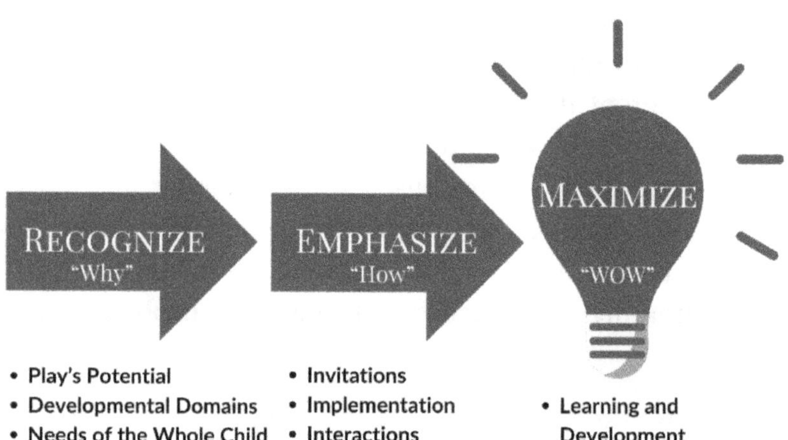

If I've *recognized* that a child I'm guiding is working on entering play situations and taking turns with friends, then I'm going to *emphasize* some of those key skills as I invite, implement, and interact in the play activities coming up. I may plan more games and open activities that lend themselves to turn-taking. I may scaffold some social situations in a way that model and support this child in asking friends to play or negotiating turn-taking. That's the difference between playing duck-duck-goose because it's "cute" and playing duck-duck-goose because I know it will support the child's development. When we know our WHY, it changes everything about WHAT we choose and HOW we do it. I recognize the objectives and opportunities so I can emphasize the right types of support in order to maximize those learning opportunities for children.

And that's what we want for the children we work with—the best opportunities to learn in the way they were meant to. As much as I love play and love being an "advocate for play," I sometimes bristle at the term. I am first an advocate for children, and I know play is a critical part of their optimal development. I don't support play because there's some noble cause in supporting play itself. I support play because play supports children. And helping children and families receive responsive, respectful support in these critical, precious early years IS a noble cause.

Thank you for being a part of it.

Key Takeaways:

- **Play and learning** are not separate—play is a powerful method for deeper learning.
- The most effective learning environments balance **child-led exploration and active discovery** with **intentional adult guidance**.

Reflect:

- **Why** does active discovery lead to deeper learning than direct instruction alone? When have you observed this?
- **How** have your students/children responded to invitations in your learning environment? How could you improve your invitations?
- **How** do you know when you've reached that *just right* balance of freedom and support, as described in the metaphor of the swing?

Take Action:

- **Share** the research on active discovery and guided play with a colleague or parent.
- Use the **Recognize-Emphasize-Maximize** framework in your planning this week.

CONCLUSION

All Children Deserve Play

Despite the overwhelming body of research showing that play fuels deep learning, some schools have mistakenly pushed it aside in the name of academic rigor.

That word, rigor, gets thrown around a lot in education today, but sometimes I wonder if we're all on the same page when it comes to what it actually means. (As Inigo Montoya famously says in *The Princess Bride*, "You keep using that word. I do not think it means what you think it means.") Rigor has been invoked to explain why some schools are ditching recess, packing away the blocks and dramatic play centers, and assigning hours of homework to young children, but none of that automatically equates with actual rigor.

After perusing several dictionaries for guidance on the word's definition, I determined that my preferred definition of rigor implies the thorough practice of something. There are other definitions, of course, and they include less-palatable perspectives, such as rigor mortis or words like severe or extreme. Given the range of meanings—and my personal preference to avoid linking early education to death or extremity—I'd argue that the best educational interpretation of rigor is "thorough." Yet, sometimes, when I hear something passed off in the name of rigor, it's actually quite superficial. Things like flashcards and worksheets and standardized testing.

Too often, rigor has come to mean less instead of more—less play, less art, less social interaction—all in the name of having more "rigor." But a rigorous, thorough early childhood education addresses the needs of the whole child. It applies concepts and discoveries to many different areas and forms. A thorough education allows children time and space to wonder and be curious and to sink into the process of actively questioning and exploring and creating understanding together.

True academic rigor isn't about stripping away joy, agency, and exploration—it's about embracing them as the foundation of deep learning. It's important for all children to have access to a truly rigorous education, one that is active, engaging, meaningful, social, iterative, and joyful;

one that applies the science of learning.[1] They all deserve an education where they can dive deep, investigate new ideas and get hands-on. It's another reason why young children need play.

The Misguided Narrative of "Catching Up"

In my work speaking to and training early childhood teams across the United States, I've had the opportunity to observe and discuss programs in many different regions serving many different demographics. Regardless of the various differences, there's an interesting and, quite frankly, disturbing thread that emerges. Generally, play is understood to be important for young children. That is, until those children are viewed as "behind," or needing to "catch up," or until adults become eager for those children to somehow "get ahead."

Most often, these children are already at a disadvantage economically, developmentally, or academically. In these instances, it's common to find grown-ups who say "these kids" don't need play, or only need it as an occasional break when the work is done. But play is the very tool that research supports as the most effective for helping them "catch up."

In an interview with NPR, Dr. Farran from the Tennessee pre-K study noted:

"One of the biases that I hadn't examined in myself is the idea that poor children need a different sort of preparation from children of higher-income families...

Higher-income families are not choosing this kind of preparation."[2]

She noted that children whose families have the means to be selective are generally more likely to choose programs that are more child-centered and rooted in play. However, when it comes to the programs created for low-income families by the state, the strategy is likely to include a disproportionate amount of worksheets, flashcards, and direct instruction. There is more time spent in whole group instruction where children are more likely to be talked *to* than talked *with*, and an outsized amount of time in transitions, simply moving children around an equally outsized facility, one that was likely designed for children twice their age.

Erika Christakis, a distinguished early childhood educator, author, and commentator, has made a similar observation. In her book, *The Importance of Being Little*, she writes:

"The young children who need active play-based learning the most are usually the ones who are least likely to get it from preschool... Society's message seems to be that these kooky, hands-on experiences are nice for affluent children, but the poor and disadvantaged ones need the 'real' teaching."[3]

"Indeed, they do," she writes, explaining that's precisely the problem.

The children who logically need the "best" educational environment in order to "catch up" are often the ones who get more of what research tells us *doesn't* work effectively: too much whole group instruction, excessive transition times, flashcards, worksheets, direct instruction, and rote memorization.

It's interesting to me that the data often referenced to support play-based, high-quality early childhood education, data that show long-term positive benefits, are often derived from studies that have been done with disadvantaged populations. Yet the methods that they support are often more easily found among affluent children.

To name just a few examples, the Abecedarian and Perry Preschool projects were intentionally focused on underserved children in an effort to disrupt intergenerational poverty. Pioneers in the early education field like Montessori and Vygotsky, established their work demonstrating the benefits of their methods in populations that had, in many regards, been excluded from education or even thought of as unteachable. Their pupils were the children who supposedly couldn't "catch up." They proved everyone wrong when these children were supported with active, hands-on, playful learning techniques.

But who is more likely to have access to programs inspired by the work of Montessori and Vygotsky or that look similar to the Abecedarian or Perry Preschool projects today? Affluent children. And this disadvantage may be magnified as many urban and underserved areas may not only have less play in their school programs but also less accessible play spaces in their homes and communities outside of school. There are some who believe that those who are "behind" or "disadvantaged" or considered "other" in some way need more flashcards and worksheets and drilling to catch up to the affluent children who are more likely to be...playing. The dissonance is rather astounding.

Whether children are disadvantaged economically or due to physical or developmental challenges, some may argue that "these children," they're the ones that need to buckle down and "catch up." "Play is nice," they may say. "It's cute, but we'll have to save it for later. *These kids* have work to do. They need to catch up." But why would we expect them to "catch up" if we're not supporting them in a way that we know contributes to healthy and effective growth and development? Why would children be expected to "catch up" when we're giving them more of what doesn't work? What's more, this "catching-up" argument can go down a slippery slope very quickly.

Falling Behind?

Unfortunately, more advantaged children are not always immune to these pressures. In addition to programs targeting affluent families with the narrative that they need to make sure they aren't wasting their child's potential and should help them "get ahead," the disruption of the COVID pandemic has now cast a shadow over all children, implying they ALL need to "catch up."

The United States' report card for 2024 was delivered by the National Assessment of Educational Progress

(NAEP) at the end of January, 2025, and showed that, for the most part, the percentage of students scoring at or above a basic level in math and reading has continued to drop for 4th and 8th graders, a trend that began before 2020 but was greatly exacerbated by the context of the pandemic.[4] Released five years after that cataclysmic disruption, the new report showed the percentage of 8th graders scoring at or above the basic range for reading skills had hit the lowest point in over 30 years, and 4th grade levels were threatening to do the same. According to the national report, 30-40% of the students assessed failed to score at a basic level for reading skills. The share of students meeting or exceeding the basic benchmark in math provided only slightly better news, with a minor uptick for 4th graders, still placing them behind their pre-pandemic counterparts, and 8th graders' rates stagnating.

In response to this somber report, the US Department of Education stated in a press release dated January 29, 2025:

"Today's NAEP results reveal a heartbreaking reality for American students and confirm our worst fears: not only did most students not recover from pandemic-related learning loss, but those students who were the most behind and needed the most support have fallen even further behind... We must do better for our students."[5]

Essentially, as a nation, all children have been deemed "behind," particularly since the pandemic. It's true that we can, and must, do better for all children. But sometimes when adults say they just want to help in the worst way possible, they unintentionally end up helping in the *worst* way possible.

Even if we accept the label of "behind" (which is a whole other discussion), what are our youngest learners behind *on*? What have they had less of or missed out on?

Young children who are in early childhood programs today were infants and toddlers during the pandemic. They did not miss out on flashcards and worksheets and recitations. It's not likely they had less time with technology than their earlier counterparts. They did not miss out on rote memorization or walking silently through hallways without talking. These are not the things that will help them "catch up."

More likely than not, if they're behind on anything, they're "behind" on the number of interactions they've had with a range of caring adults. They may be "behind" on the number of hours they've played in group settings or the amount of practice they've had negotiating social challenges. They may be "behind" on the number of relationships they've built with peers and adults in their wider community. They might have amassed fewer conversational turns and been part of fewer meaningful language experiences. Perhaps, they're "behind" on the opportunities they had to get hands-on with their environment in a time when the world became fixated on avoiding contact. Or maybe they had fewer opportunities to tackle hard tasks independently or take on healthy risks while all the adults in their lives were in protection mode. So, the argument that our youngest children are behind because of COVID is, in reality, an argument that they may actually need *more* play.

And if you were to push back at this point and, rightly, note that diminishing performances had begun even before the pandemic, and that the societal impacts of COVID simply sped up a decline that was already in motion, I would then say you're very observant. And that the answer for our youngest learners is still play.

Play as a Priority

In his popular book, *The Anxious Generation*, psychologist, professor, and author, Jonathan Haidt chronicles what he calls "the great rewiring of childhood," which coincides with these earlier declines in both learning and wellness markers.[6] Speaking about the book at an NYU event, he noted, "We've had a play-based childhood for literally 200 million years because we're mammals and all mammals play. That's how we wired up our brains. Somewhere in the 1990s, it stopped—and stopped dead by 2010. It faded away and was replaced, very suddenly, by the phone-based childhood between 2010 and 2015."[7]

Dr. Haidt emphasizes that the intrusion of screens into childhood has pushed out play, creating "experience blockers," a dangerous proposition for development and learning. It may be tempting to think that we build brains with information, and that tablets, apps, videos, and whatever other delivery model is the key to helping young learners "catch up." But it takes more than information inputs to build young brains.

Experience is actually what drives development. Information has its place, of course, but information alone doesn't drive development. In a rapidly advancing technological world, we must remember that we can't pre-program development, script it into a video, or hand it over to AI. Real development requires real experience. Real development requires real relationships. Real development requires play.

So, for which children should we prioritize play? With all the research and all the data right in front of us, who would we decide are the "other" children this information doesn't actually apply to? There are no "other kids" in this scenario. This book is about all children. All children need play. All children benefit from play. All children deserve play.

Due to the varied pressures of today, "all kids" are now at risk of poor practice in our early education settings. There are too many adults with the best of intentions but terrible information, who are unfortunately pushing pressures down—and pushing play out. We don't help children thrive by doubling down on what doesn't work. To create the best learning environments for young children, we need more than just good intentions—we need solid, research-backed information guiding our decisions.

The intention of this book is to give you that solid information. And if you're reading it, I believe you're full of good intentions. Now, it's time for all of us to take our good information and good intentions and put them to work.

Play isn't optional. It's essential. And every child—no matter their background—deserves it. The good news? We have the knowledge to make that happen. Now, it's time to act.

Our children are counting on us.

Key Takeaways:

- True academic **rigor** includes play. It's an essential component of **deep, meaningful** education.
- Children labeled as "**behind**" are often deprived of the very learning experiences—like play—that research shows help them the most.
- Adults pushing for more structured, test-driven early learning often have the best intentions but operate on misinformation. **It's time to align practice with research.**

Reflect:

- **How** has your own definition of "rigor" in education evolved?
- **What** barriers to play-based learning exist in your setting, and how might they be overcome?

Take Action:

- **Share** research on the importance of play with administrators, parents, and policymakers to ensure decisions are grounded in evidence.
- **Identify** one concrete way you can increase meaningful play opportunities in your learning environment and take action to implement it.

Notes

Chapter One

1. Lipsey, M. W., Farran, D. C., & Durkin, K. (2018).

2. "Fadeout effect" is the term used to describe diminishing positive impacts of attending a program as nonattenders catch up after a short amount of time.

   See also:
   Magnuson, K. A., Ruhm, C., & Waldfogel, J. (2007); McCormick, M., Weiland, C., Hsueh, J., Pralica, M., Weissman, A. K., Moffett, L., Snow, C., & Sachs, J. (2021)

3. Durkin, K., Lipsey, M. W., Farran, D. C., & Wiesen, S. E. (2022).

4. Morgan, A. (2024, January 4).

5. Kamenetz, A. (2022, February 10).

6. Morgan, A. (2024, January 4).

   This episode with Dr. Dale Farran (Episode 64) is a must-listen for those who want to understand the research around the Tennessee pre-K research. It pairs well with Episode 50, which dives into the popular NPR article on the study by Kamenetz, A. (2022, February 10).

7. Yoshikawa, H., Weiland, C., Brooks-Gunn, J., Burchinal, M., Espinosa, L., Gormley, W., Ludwig, J., Magnuson, K., Phillips, D., & Zaslow, M. (2013).

8. It's important to note that Tennessee has since adjusted their pre-K program.

9. Whitaker, A., Burchinal, M., Jenkins, J., Bailey, D., Watts, T., Duncan, G., Hart, E., & Peisner-Feinberg, E. (2023).

Chapter Two

1. As another example of the principle, "people don't value what they don't understand," consider this anecdote shared in Green (2014). When A&W launched a 1/3 pound hamburger patty to compete with McDonald's quarter-pounder, it failed. Why? Because Americans generally believed that 1/3 was smaller than 1/4. People don't value what they don't understand. Which, in this case, was fractions.

2. Morgan, A (2024, June 8).

Chapter Three

1. Gray, P. (2017).

   See also:
   Gray, P. (2023, April 25).

2. Gray, P., Lancy, D. F., & Bjorklund, D. F. (2023).

3. Yenigun, S. (2014, August 6).

4. Zosh, J. M., Hirsh-Pasek, K., Hopkins, E. J., Jensen, H., Liu, C., Neale, D., Solis, S. L., & Whitebread, D. (2018).

   See also:
   Zosh, J.M., Gaudreau, C., Golinkoff, R. M., Hirsh-Pasek, K. (2022).

5. Weisberg, D. S., Hirsh-Pasek, K., Golinkoff, R. M., Kittredge, A. K., & Klahr, D. (2016).

   See Also:
   Skene, K., O'Farrelly, C. M., Byrne, E. M., Kirby, N., Stevens, E. C., & Ramchandani, P. G. (2022); Weisberg, D. S., Hirsh-Pasek, K., & Golinkoff, R. M. (2013).

Chapter Four

1. Yogman, M., Garner, A., Hutchinson, J., Hirsh-Pasek, K., & Golinkoff, R. M. (2018).

2. Wang, S., & Aamodt, S. (2012).

3. Gray, P., Lancy, D. F., & Bjorklund, D. F. (2023).

4. Phillips, J. M., & Gully, S. M. (1997).

5. Hovenkamp-Hermelink, J. H. M., Jeronimus, B. F., van der Veen, D. C., Spinhoven, P., Penninx, B. W. J. H., Schoevers, R. A., & Riese, H. (2019).

6. Leotti, L. A., Iyengar, S. S., & Ochsner, K. N. (2010). Emphasis added.

7. Bandura, A. (1977).

   Bandura's Social Learning Theory suggests that children build confidence, self-efficacy, and resilience as they master increasingly challenging tasks. This is best accomplished as they take on risks in a social environment where they are supported, encouraged, and scaffolded by caring peers and adults.

8. Dodd, H. F., & Lester, K. J. (2021).

9. Gray, P. (2011).

Chapter Five

1. Conti, G., Heckman, J. J., & Pinto, R. (2016).

2. Heckman, J. J., & Karapakula, G. (2019, May 30).

3. Whitaker, A., Burchinal, M., Jenkins, J. M., Bailey, D. H., Watts, T. W., Duncan, G. J., Hart, E. R., & Peisner-Feinberg, E. S. (2023).

4. Farran, D. (2022, February 12).

5. McCormick, M., Weiland, C., Hsueh, J., Pralica, M., Weissman, A. K., Moffett, L., Snow, C., & Sachs, J. (2021).

6. Evidence from Romeo et al. (2021) as well as van der Veen et al. (2017) demonstrate that brain growth and content learning are enhanced by conversational turns and classroom dialogue, respectively. In spite of this, Bassok et al (2016) identifies the trend for an increase in whole group instruction in early childhood settings, while Farran (2016) shows whole group instruction replaced free choice time as the most common instructional strategy for federal grant pre-K programs, in spite of the fact that this didactic approach is less effective.

7. McCormick, M., Weiland, C., Hsueh, J., Pralica, M., Weissman, A. K., Moffett, L., Snow, C., & Sachs, J. (2021).

8. Gordon, N. S., Burke, S., Akil, H., Watson, S. J., & Panksepp, J. (2003).

9. Brown, S. L., & Vaughan, C. C. (2009).

10. Willis, J. (2014, July 18).

11. Vogel, S., Kluen, L. M., Fernández, G., & Schwabe, L. (2018).

12. Shah, P., Weeks, H., Richards, B., & Kaciroti, N. (2018).

13. Berliner, W. (2020, January 28).

14. Chouinard, M. M., Harris, P. L., & Maratsos, M. P. (2007).

15. Engel, S. (2011).

Chapter Six

1. Rule, J., Goddu, M. K., Chu, J., Pinter, V., Reagan, E. R., Bonawitz, E., ... Ullman, T. D. (2023, July 9).

2. Jones, D. E., Greenberg, M., & Crowley, M. (2015).

3. Gilliam, W. S., & Shahar, G. (2006).

   See also:
   Gilliam, W. (2005).

4. This rate may be higher today and is markedly higher for preschoolers with disabilities when compared to their peers.
   See also:

Zeng, S., Pereira, B., Larson, A., Corr, C. P., O'Grady, C., & Stone-MacDonald, A. (2020).

5. Gilliam, W. (2009, June 16).

6. Bassok, D., Latham, S., & Rorem, A. (2016).

7. Granted, one study is looking at the preschool years while the other is examining kindergarten, but I do believe they are representative of shifts that span across the early childhood spectrum.

8. Gray-Lobe, G., Pathak, P. A., & Walters, C. (2021).

9. Gopnik, A. (2021, May 27). Emphasis added.

Chapter Seven

1. Gopnik, A. (2019, October 11). Emphasis added.

2. Piazza, E. A., Hasenfratz, L., Hasson, U., & Lew-Williams, C. (2019).

3. Phillips, D., Lipsey, M., Dodge, K., Haskins, R., Bassok, D., Burchinal, M., Duncan, G., Dynarski, M., & Magnuson, K. (2017).

Chapter Eight

1. Sobel, D. M., & Sommerville, J. A. (2010).

2. Bonawitz, E., Shafto, P., Gweon, H., Goodman, N. D., Spelke, E., & Schulz, L. (2011).

3. Fisher, K. R., Hirsh-Pasek, K., Newcombe, N., & Golinkoff, R. M. (2013).

4. Weisberg, D. S., Hirsh-Pasek, K., Golinkoff, R. M., Kittredge, A. K., & Klahr, D. (2016).

5. Zosh, J. M., Hirsh-Pasek, K., Hopkins, E. J., Jensen, H., Liu, C., Neale, D., Solis, S. L., & Whitebread, D. (2018).

Conclusion

1. Zosh, J. M., Hirsh-Pasek, K., Hopkins, E. J., Jensen, H., Liu, C., Neale, D., Solis, S. L., & Whitebread, D. (2018).

   See also:
   Nesbitt, K. T., Hirsh-Pasek, K., Golinkoff, R. M., & Blinkoff, E. (2023).

2. Kamenetz, A. (2022, February 10).

3. Christakis, E. (2016).

4. U.S. Department of Education, Institute of Education Sciences, National Center for Education Statistics, National Assessment of Educational Progress (NAEP). (2025).

See also:
Barnum, M., Randazzo, S. (2025).

5. U.S. Department of Education. (2025, January 29).

6. Haidt, J. (2024).

7. Hollander, J. (2024).

Bibliography

Bandura, A. (1977). Self-efficacy: Toward a unifying theory of behavioral change. *Psychological Review, 84*(2), 191–215. https://doi.org/10.1037/0033-295X.84.2.191

Barnum, M., & Randazzo, S. (2025, January 30). Reading Skills Fall Further in New School Test Scores. *The Wall Street Journal*, A3. https://www.wsj.com/us-news/education/reading-test-scores-american-students-5fb78d4e

Bassok, D., Latham, S., & Rorem, A. (2016). Is Kindergarten the New First Grade? *AERA Open*, *2*(1), 233285841561635. https://doi.org/10.1177/2332858415616358

Berliner, W. (2020, January 28). "Schools are killing curiosity": why we need to stop telling children to shut up and learn. *The Guardian*. https://www.theguardian.com/education/2020/jan/28/schools-killing-curiosity-learn

Bonawitz, E., Shafto, P., Gweon, H., Goodman, N. D., Spelke, E., & Schulz, L. (2011). The double-edged sword of pedagogy:

Instruction limits spontaneous exploration and discovery. *Cognition*, *120*(3), 322–330. https://doi.org/10.1016/j.cognition.2010.10.001

Brown, S. L., & Vaughan, C. C. (2009). *Play: How it Shapes the Brain, Opens the Imagination, and Invigorates the Soul.* Avery.

Chouinard, M. M., Harris, P. L., & Maratsos, M. P. (2007). Children's questions: A mechanism for cognitive development. *Monographs of the Society for Research in Child Development*, *72*(1), 1–129. https://doi.org/10.1111/j.1540-5834.2007.00413.x

Christakis, E. (2016). *The importance of being little: what young children really need from grownups*. Penguin Books, An Imprint of Penguin Random House LLC.

Conti, G., Heckman, J. J., & Pinto, R. (2016). The Effects of Two Influential Early Childhood Interventions on Health and Healthy Behaviour. *The Economic Journal*, 126(596), F28–F65. https://doi.org/10.1111/ecoj.12420

Dodd, H. F., & Lester, K. J. (2021). Adventurous Play as a Mechanism for Reducing Risk for Childhood Anxiety: A Conceptual Model. *Clinical Child and Family Psychology Review*, *24*(1). https://doi.org/10.1007/s10567-020-00338-w

Durkin, K., Lipsey, M. W., Farran, D. C., & Wiesen, S. E. (2022). Effects of a statewide pre-kindergarten program on children's achievement and behavior through sixth grade. *Developmental Psychology*, *58*(3). https://doi.org/10.1037/dev0001301

Engel, S. (2011). Children's Need to Know: Curiosity in Schools. *Harvard Educational Review, 81*(4), 625–645. https://doi.org/10.17763/haer.81.4.h054131316473115

Farran, D. C. (2016, July 14). *Federal Preschool Development Grants: Evaluation needed.* Brookings. https://www.brookings.edu/articles/federal-preschool-development-grants-evaluation-needed/

Farran, D. (2022, February 12). *Early Developmental Competencies: Or Why Pre-K Does Not Have Lasting Effects.* Defending the Early Years. https://dey.org/early-developmental-competencies-or-why-pre-k-does-not-have-lasting-effects/

Gilliam, W. (2005). Prekindergarteners Left Behind: Expulsion Rates in State Prekindergarten Programs Background. In *FCD Policy Brief, Series No. 3.* https://www.fcd-us.org/wp-content/uploads/2016/04/ExpulsionPolicyBrief.pdf

Gilliam, W. (2009, June 16). *Demonstrating the Links between Research, Practice & Policy in Early Childhood Mental Health.* Presentation given at Office of Applied Research 18th National Institute for Early Childhood Professional Development Charlotte, North Carolina. https://www.slideserve.com/ronia/demonstrating-the-links-between-research-practice-policy-in-early-childhood-mental-health

Fisher, K. R., Hirsh-Pasek, K., Newcombe, N., & Golinkoff, R. M. (2013). Taking Shape: Supporting Preschoolers' Acquisition of Geometric Knowledge Through Guided Play. *Child Development, 84*(6), 1872–1878. https://doi.org/10.1111/cdev.12091

Gilliam, W. S., & Shahar, G. (2006). Preschool and child care expulsion and suspension: Rates and predictors in one state. *Infants & Young Children, 19* (3), 228–245. https://doi.org/10.1097/00001163-200607000-00007

Gopnik, A. (2019, October 11). The Ultimate Learning Machines. *The Wall Street Journal.* https://www.wsj.com/articles/the-ultimate-learning-machines-11570806023

Gopnik, A. (2021, May 27). Preschool's 'Sleeper Effect' on Later Life. *The Wall Street Journal.* https://www.wsj.com/articles/preschools-sleeper-effect-on-later-life-11622146543

Gordon, N. S., Burke, S., Akil, H., Watson, S. J., & Panksepp, J. (2003). Socially-induced brain "fertilization": play promotes brain derived neurotrophic factor transcription in the amygdala and dorsolateral frontal cortex in juvenile rats. *Neuroscience Letters, 341*(1), 17–20. https://doi.org/10.1016/s0304-3940(03)00158-7

Gray, P. (2011). The Decline of Play and the Rise of Psychopathology in Children and Adolescents. https://files.eric.ed.gov/fulltext/EJ985541.pdf

Gray, P. (2017). What Exactly Is Play, and Why Is It Such a Powerful Vehicle for Learning? *Topics in Language Disorders, 37*(3), 217–228. https://doi.org/10.1097/tld.0000000000000130

Gray, P. (2023, April 25). *#2. What Exactly Is Play?* Play Makes Us Human. https://petergray.substack.com/p/2-what-exactly-is-this-thing-we-call

Gray, P., Lancy, D. F., & Bjorklund, D. F. (2023). Decline in independent activity as a cause of decline in children's mental well-being: Summary of the evidence. *The Journal of Pediatrics, 260,* 113352. https://doi.org/10.1016/j.jpeds.2023.02.004

Gray-Lobe, G., Pathak, P. A., & Walters, C. (2021). The Long-Term Effects of Universal Preschool in Boston. *SSRN Electronic Journal, Policy Brief.* https://doi.org/10.2139/ssrn.3842731

Green, E. (2014, July 23). Why Do Americans Stink at Math? *The New York Times.* https://www.nytimes.com/2014/07/27/magazine/why-do-americans-stink-at-math.html

Haidt, J. (2024). *The Anxious Generation: How the Great Rewiring of Childhood Is Causing an Epidemic of Mental Illness.* Penguin.

Heckman, J. J., & Karapakula, G. (2019, May 30). *Intergenerational and Intragenerational Externalities of the Perry Preschool Project.* National Bureau of Economic Research Working Paper Series. https://www.nber.org/papers/w25889

Hollander, J. (2024). *"The Great Rewiring of Childhood."* Nyu.edu. https://www.nyu.edu/about/news-publications/news/2024/june/-the-great-rewiring-of-childhood-.html

Hovenkamp-Hermelink, J. H. M., Jeronimus, B. F., van der Veen, D. C., Spinhoven, P., Penninx, B. W. J. H., Schoevers, R. A., & Riese, H. (2019). Differential associations of locus of control with anxiety, depression and life-events: A five-wave, nine-year study to test stability and change. *Journal of Affective Disorders, 253,* 26–34. https://doi.org/10.1016/j.jad.2019.04.005

Jones, D. E., Greenberg, M., & Crowley, M. (2015). Early Social-Emotional Functioning and Public Health: The Relationship Between Kindergarten Social Competence and Future Wellness. *American Journal of Public Health, 105*(11), 2283–2290. https://doi.org/10.2105/ajph.2015.302630

Kamenetz, A. (2022, February 10). A top researcher says it's time to rethink our entire approach to preschool. *NPR.* https://www.npr.org/2022/02/10/1079406041/researcher-says-rethink-prek-preschool-prekindergarten

Leotti, L. A., Iyengar, S. S., & Ochsner, K. N. (2010). Born to choose: The origins and value of the need for control. *Trends in Cognitive Sciences,* 14(10), 457–463. https://doi.org/10.1016/j.tics.2010.08.001

Lipsey, M. W., Farran, D. C., & Durkin, K. (2018). Effects of the Tennessee Prekindergarten Program on children's achievement and behavior through third grade. *Early Childhood Research Quarterly, 45,* 155–176. https://doi.org/10.1016/j.ecresq.2018.03.005

Magnuson, K. A., Ruhm, C., & Waldfogel, J. (2007). The persistence of preschool effects: Do subsequent classroom experiences matter? *Early Childhood Research Quarterly, 22*(1), 18–38. https://doi.org/10.1016/j.ecresq.2006.10.002

McCormick, M., Weiland, C., Hsueh, J., Pralica, M., Weissman, A. K., Moffett, L., Snow, C., & Sachs, J. (2021). Is Skill Type the Key to the PreK Fadeout Puzzle? Differential Associations Between Enrollment in PreK and

Constrained and Unconstrained Skills Across Kindergarten. *Child Development, 92*(4). https://doi.org/10.1111/cdev.13520

Morgan, A. (Host). (2024, January 4). Episode 61: Getting Curious About PreK Research (with Dr. Dale Farran) [Audio podcast episode]. In *Not Just Cute: The Podcast.* https://notjustcute.com/podcast/episode61/

Morgan, A. (Host). (2024, June 8). Episode 75: Empowering Parents as Teachers—Mobile Early Education Outreach Team (with Play Smart Literacy) [Audio podcast episode]. In *Not Just Cute: The Podcast.* https://notjustcute.com/podcast/episode75

Nesbitt, K. T., Hirsh-Pasek, K., Golinkoff, R. M., & Blinkoff, E. (2023). Making schools work: An equation for active playful learning. *Theory into Practice, 62*(2). https://doi.org/10.1080/00405841.2023.2202136

Phillips, D., Lipsey, M., Dodge, K., Haskins, R., Bassok, D., Burchinal, M., Duncan, G., Dynarski, M., & Magnuson, K. (2017). *Puzzling it Out: The Current State of Scientific Knowledge on Pre-Kindergarten Effects, A Consensus Statement.* Brookings Institution. https://www.brookings.edu/wp-content/uploads/2017/04/consensus-statement_final.pdf

Phillips, J. M., & Gully, S. M. (1997). Role of goal orientation, ability, need for achievement, and locus of control in the self-efficacy and goal-setting process. *Journal of Applied Psychology, 82*(5), 792–802. https://doi.org/10.1037/0021-9010.82.5.792

Piazza, E. A., Hasenfratz, L., Hasson, U., & Lew-Williams, C. (2019). Infant and Adult Brains Are Coupled to the Dynamics of Natural Communication. *Psychological Science, 31*(1), 6–17. https://doi.org/10.1177/0956797619878698

Romeo, R. R., Leonard, J. A., Grotzinger, H. M., Robinson, S. T., Takada, M. E., Mackey, A. P., Scherer, E., Rowe, M. L., West, M. R., & Gabrieli, J. D. E. (2021). Neuroplasticity associated with changes in conversational turn-taking following a family-based intervention. *Developmental Cognitive Neuroscience, 49*, 100967. https://doi.org/10.1016/j.dcn.2021.100967

Rule, J., Goddu, M. K., Chu, J., Pinter, V., Reagan, E. R., Bonawitz, E., ... Ullman, T. D. (2023, July 9). Fun isn't easy: Children selectively manipulate task difficulty when "playing for fun" vs. "playing to win". (Preprint) https://doi.org/10.31234/osf.io/q7wh4

Shah, P., Weeks, H., Richards, B., & Kaciroti, N. (2018). Early Childhood Curiosity and Kindergarten Reading and Math Academic Achievement. *Pediatric Research*. 84. 10.1038/s41390-018-0039-3.

Skene, K., O'Farrelly, C. M., Byrne, E. M., Kirby, N., Stevens, E. C., & Ramchandani, P. G. (2022). Can guidance during play enhance children's learning and development in educational contexts? A systematic review and meta-analysis. *Child Development, 93*(4). https://doi.org/10.1111/cdev.13730

Sobel, D. M., & Sommerville, J. A. (2010). The Importance of Discovery in Children's Causal Learning from

Interventions. *Frontiers in Psychology, 1.* https://doi.org/10.3389/fpsyg.2010.00176

U.S. Department of Education, Institute of Education Sciences, National Center for Education Statistics, National Assessment of Educational Progress (NAEP). (2025). NAEP Long-Term Trend Assessment Results: Reading and Mathematics. Washington, DC: National Center for Education Statistics. Retrieved 2025 from https://www.nationsreportcard.gov/

U.S. Department of Education. (2025, January 29). *U.S. Department of Education Issues Statement on the Nation's Report Card.* U.S. Department of Education. https://www.ed.gov/about/news/press-release/us-department-of-education-issues-statement-nations-report-card

van der Veen, C., de Mey, J. R. P. B., van Kruistum, C. J., & van Oers, B. (2017). The effect of productive classroom talk and metacommunication on young children's oral communicative competence and subject matter knowledge: An intervention study in early childhood education. *Learning and Instruction*, 48, 14-22. https://doi.org/10.1016/j.learninstruc.2016.06.001

Vogel, S., Kluen, L. M., Fernández, G., & Schwabe, L. (2018). Stress affects the neural ensemble for integrating new information and prior knowledge. *NeuroImage*, *173*, 176–187. https://doi.org/10.1016/j.neuroimage.2018.02.03

Wang, S., & Aamodt, S. (2012). Play, Stress, and the Learning Brain. *Cerebrum: The Dana Forum on Brain Science, 2012*, 12. https://pmc.ncbi.nlm.nih.gov/articles/PMC3574776/

Weisberg, D. S., Hirsh-Pasek, K., & Golinkoff, R. M. (2013). Guided Play: Where Curricular Goals Meet a Playful Pedagogy. *Mind, Brain, and Education, 7*(2), 104–112. https://doi.org/10.1111/mbe.12015

Weisberg, D. S., Hirsh-Pasek, K., Golinkoff, R. M., Kittredge, A. K., & Klahr, D. (2016). Guided Play: Principles and Practices. *Current Directions in Psychological Science, 25*(3), 177–182. https://doi.org/10.1177/0963721416645512

Whitaker, A., Burchinal, M., Jenkins, J., Bailey, D., Watts, T., Duncan, G., Hart, E., & Peisner-Feinberg, E. (2023). Why are Preschool Programs Becoming Less Effective? (EdWorkingPaper: 23-885). Retrieved from Annenberg Institute at Brown University: https://doi.org/10.26300/smqa-n695

Willis, J. (2014, July 18). The Neuroscience Behind Stress and Learning. *Edutopia.* https://www.edutopia.org/article/blog-neuroscience-behind-stress-and-learning-judy-willis/

Yenigun, S. (2014, August 6). *Play Doesn't End With Childhood: Why Adults Need Recess Too.* NPR.org. https://www.npr.org/sections/ed/2014/08/06/336360521/play-doesnt-end-with-childhood-why-adults-need-recess-too

Yogman, M., Garner, A., Hutchinson, J., Hirsh-Pasek, K., & Golinkoff, R. M. (2018). The Power of play: a Pediatric Role in Enhancing Development in Young Children. *Pediatrics, 142*(3). https://doi.org/10.1542/peds.2018-2058

Yoshikawa, H., Weiland, C., Brooks-Gunn, J., Burchinal, M., Espinosa, L., Gormley, W., Ludwig, J., Magnuson, K., Phillips, D., & Zaslow, M. (2013). *Investing in Our Future: The Evidence Base on Preschool Education.* https://www.fcd-us.org/wp-content/uploads/2016/04/Evidence-Base-on-Preschool-Education-FINAL.pdf

Zeng, S., Pereira, B., Larson, A., Corr, C. P., O'Grady, C., & Stone-MacDonald, A. (2020). Preschool Suspension and Expulsion for Young Children with Disabilities. *Exceptional Children, 87*(2), 001440292094983. https://doi.org/10.1177/0014402920949832

Zosh, J.M., Gaudreau, C., Golinkoff, R. M., Hirsh-Pasek, K. (2022). The Power of Playful Learning in the Early Childhood Setting. In NAEYC. (2022). *Developmentally Appropriate Practice In Early Childhood Programs Serving Children From Birth... Through Age 8, Fourth Edition.* National Association for the Education of Young Children.

Zosh, J. M., Hirsh-Pasek, K., Hopkins, E. J., Jensen, H., Liu, C., Neale, D., Solis, S. L., & Whitebread, D. (2018). Accessing the Inaccessible: Redefining Play as a Spectrum. *Frontiers in Psychology,* 9(1124). https://doi.org/10.3389/fpsyg.2018.01124

Acknowledgements

About 25 years ago, I was a graduate student at Utah State University. In the years since then, I've often reflected on how my experiences there have shaped the rest of my life. Not least among them were my experiences at the Adele and Dale Young Child Development Laboratory School with my mentors, Dr. Shelley Knudsen Lindauer and Farol Nelson, and my cohort bestie, Kelli Barker. What I learned from these women, and those formative experiences, has shaped how I think and how I do this work. I will forever be grateful.

The second group to shape this particular work was the directors and team leaders who participated in the beta program for my *Powerful Play Foundations* course. As the materials rolled out, their passion for this work and this message—and their requests for a way to share it beyond their own teams, with parents, admin, decision makers, and others—inspired this book. Thank you for your encouragement and for the work you do every day.

Enormous gratitude goes to a long list of people who encouraged me to write a book. It took me so long to get around to it that I'm sure to miss someone who offered encouragement along that long and winding road. Those dream-stokers include (but certainly aren't limited to): Nollie Haws, Triné Nelson, Jill Riley, Cassidy Sugimoto, Marlene Bosanko Cline, Trisha Deming, Allison McDonald, Vanessa Levin, Cindy Theel, Michele Borba, Rae Pica, Janet Lansbury, Bryan Pratt, and Dennis and Julie Galvon. Also, to Paije Abplanalp—in lieu of her top fan trophy (though shipping and handling fees may still apply☺).

I'm deeply appreciative of the countless researchers who are devoted to the relentless pursuit of truth through the disciplined and principled application of the scientific process. These professionals spend years empirically answering questions many of us—if we even manage to ask them—are often confidently wrong in assuming we already know the answers to. Their data and descriptions are invaluable to society and the decision-making and policy-making processes. Some of the names of the many researchers, whose decades of work have shaped me and this book, appear in the bibliography. I am grateful to each of them—those named and unnamed. I'd like to particularly thank Kathy Hirsh Pasek for the influence of not only her academic work, but also her effervescent professionalism, as well as Dale Farran for her courage to stick with the science—even when it leads to unexpected places—and for her kindness and generosity in supporting this book and writing its foreword.

A heartfelt thank you to my own parents as well as to my in-laws—Burdette and Kathy Pratt and Vern and Carol Morgan—for teaching the value of both play and work and the reality that the two don't have to be mutually exclusive.

I'm eternally grateful to my husband, Steve, my biggest cheerleader and most patient sounding board, with whom I have had the absolute privilege of doing our most important work together—raising four amazing young men: Spencer, Will, Cole, and Wes. I'm grateful to this raucous family that will always be my happiest place, no matter where in the world they roam.

And finally, thank you to *you*—the reader. The fact that you're holding this book means you believe in the significance of childhood and the importance of doing this work well. Thank you for the time and effort you devote to serving young children and their families. Whether you're just beginning your journey or have been walking this path for decades, I'm honored to walk beside you for a little while. May this book affirm—and occasionally challenge—your instincts and beliefs, and may it ultimately inspire your next steps as we all work together to create a world where every child experiences all the joy, play, love, and learning they deserve.

About the Author

Amanda Morgan holds a dual BA in Elementary and Early Childhood Education and an MS in Human Development, with an emphasis on Child Development. She is deeply committed to supporting intentional, whole-child development through her website *Not Just Cute* and its companion podcast, *Not Just Cute: The Podcast*. With a blend of scientific insight and compelling stories, Amanda demonstrates how everyday moments—like play, relationships, and conversations—are far more than just "cute"; they're powerful tools for growth and learning. For over 15 years, she has worked with early childhood groups across the U.S. and Canada, sharing her passion and expertise as a speaker, trainer, and consultant. *Not Just Cute: How Powerful Play Drives Development in Early Childhood*, is her first book. When she's not traveling, speaking, or writing, Amanda enjoys home life with her husband and four boys a few miles from her favorite kayaking spot in Puget Sound, where she's still holding out hope for a not-too-close encounter with an orca.

If you enjoyed this book, please help others find it by sharing your review.

Find the book on Amazon, or simply scan the QR code to leave a review.

Book Amanda for your next training or event.

Whether you're planning a keynote, workshop, or full-day training, Amanda Morgan can support your team in implementing powerful, research-backed play practices with clarity and confidence.

Bring the message of *Not Just Cute* to life and equip your group with the tools and inspiration they need to elevate early learning through guided play.

Connect at notjustcute.com/speaking, or simply scan the QR code below to start the conversation.

Take the next step toward powerful play.

Powerful Play Foundations is an on-demand professional development course designed for early childhood teams ready to turn vision into action. This practical, engaging training helps teams build confident, competent, and cohesive practices rooted in guided play. It's everything you need to move from intention to implementation—together.

Learn more at notjustcute.com/powerfulplay or simply scan the QR code below.

Why We Play

"People don't value what they don't understand."

Let's help them understand play—together.

Why We Play is a set of 45 concise, reproducible letters that help you connect everyday classroom moments to the research-backed reasons behind them. Attach them to newsletters, handouts, or display boards to help families and colleagues see the purpose behind playful learning—and become advocates for it.

Explore the full collection and download **a free sample letter** at notjustcute.com/whyweplay or scan the QR code below.

www.ingramcontent.com/pod-product-compliance
Lightning Source LLC
Chambersburg PA
CBHW021146090426
42740CB00008B/962